Swift for Beginners: Learn iOS App Development from Scratch

A Complete Guide to Mastering Swift and iOS Development

BOOZMAN RICHARD

BOOKER BLUNT

All rights reserved

Table of Content

TABLE OF CONTENTS

INTRODUCTION

The Swift for beginner's iOS development landscape has evolved dramatically over the past decade, with playing a pivotal role in shaping how developers build interactive, dynamic, and scalable applications. In this rapidly changing ecosystem, staying up to date with the latest frameworks and technologies is crucial to building high-performance web applications that meet user expectations for speed, reliability, and seamless experiences across devices.

This book, *Swift for beginner's*, is designed to be your comprehensive guide to mastering the most popular iOS App development used in modern App development. Whether you are just starting your journey into App development or you're a seasoned developer looking to deepen your knowledge, this book covers everything you need to know. Each chapter is crafted to provide you with a clear understanding of the core concepts, best practices, and real-world examples, helping you build scalable, maintainable, and performant applications.

Why This Book Is Compulsory

The demand for rich, interactive web applications has never been higher. With the rise of Single Page Applications

(SPAs), Progressive Web Apps (PWAs), and mobile-first design, developers must not only understand the principles of front-end development but also leverage modern JavaScript frameworks to enhance the user experience and meet the growing demands of today's digital world.

In this book, you will:

- Gain a deep understanding of **React**, **Angular**, and **Vue.js**, each of which has its unique strengths and weaknesses.
- Learn how to implement best practices for building fast, efficient, and secure web applications.
- Dive into advanced topics such as **state management**, **routing**, **service workers**, and **performance optimization**.
- Explore real-world examples of building web apps from scratch, including integrating APIs, securing user data, and optimizing performance.
- Get hands-on experience with building **Progressive Web Apps (PWAs)**, **Single Page Applications (SPAs)**, and mobile-first web solutions.

Whether you're looking to improve your skills in building scalable front-end applications or need to stay updated with the latest trends and technologies in web development, this book will serve as your essential companion.

What You Will Learn

In the first part of the book, we'll explore the foundational concepts of JavaScript frameworks. You'll get acquainted with the core principles behind **React**, **Angular**, and **Vue.js**, including their strengths, weaknesses, and appropriate use cases. We'll dive into the fundamentals of each framework, helping you choose the right tool for your next project.

Next, we will cover how to build real-world applications with these frameworks. You'll learn how to develop powerful web apps by creating dynamic user interfaces, managing state effectively, and implementing modern features like **routing**, **authentication**, and **data binding**. You'll also get hands-on experience building **single-page applications (SPAs)** and integrating APIs to enhance the functionality of your app.

As we move deeper into advanced topics, the book will guide you through **state management** using libraries like **Redux** for React, **NgRx** for Angular, and **Vuex** for Vue.js. We'll also focus on performance optimization techniques such as **code splitting**, **lazy loading**, **caching**, and **progressive web apps (PWAs)** to ensure that your web apps perform at their best across all devices and network conditions.

Security is also a major concern when developing web applications. In this book, we'll explore how to protect your app from common vulnerabilities like **Cross-Site Scripting (XSS)**, **Cross-Site Request Forgery (CSRF)**, and **SQL Injection**. You'll learn how to implement secure authentication systems using **JWT** (JSON Web Tokens) and other modern techniques to safeguard your app's data and user privacy.

The final section of the book covers best practices and strategies for maintaining and evolving your web apps. We'll focus on **test-driven development (TDD)**, **unit testing**, and **end-to-end testing** with tools like **Jest**, **Karma**, and **Protractor**. We'll also discuss how to stay up to date with the latest trends and frameworks in the JavaScript ecosystem, ensuring your skills remain relevant in the ever-changing world of web development.

Who This Book Is For

This book is intended for developers of all experience levels who want to master modern JavaScript frameworks. Whether you are:

- A **beginner** looking to get started with React, Angular, or Vue.js, and want to learn the fundamentals of web development with modern frameworks.
- An **intermediate developer** who wants to deepen your understanding of state management, routing, testing, and performance optimization.
- An **experienced developer** seeking to stay updated on the latest tools, best practices, and trends in JavaScript frameworks, and how to build scalable, secure, and high-performance web applications.

Why Swift iOS App?

The three frameworks covered in this book—**React**, **Angular**, and **Vue.js**—are the most widely used and popular choices for building web applications today. Each framework has unique features, and understanding their strengths and use cases will help you choose the right one for your project.

- **React**: Known for its simplicity and flexibility, React is a **JavaScript library** for building user interfaces. Its component-based architecture and virtual DOM make it highly efficient for rendering dynamic UIs, and it is widely adopted for creating modern, fast web applications.
- **Angular**: Angular is a **full-fledged framework** that provides everything you need for building large-scale web applications. With built-in tools like **dependency injection**, **routing**, and **forms management**, Angular is perfect for building complex, enterprise-level apps.
- **Vue.js**: Vue is a **progressive framework** that is both easy to learn and flexible enough to scale for large applications. It combines the best features of both React and Angular, offering an approachable learning curve with powerful tools for building dynamic, modern web apps.

By the end of this book, you'll have a solid understanding of these frameworks and the ability to build robust, production-ready web apps with them.

Conclusion

The world of JavaScript frameworks is constantly evolving, and staying up-to-date with the latest tools and techniques is essential for becoming a proficient web developer. *Mastering JavaScript Frameworks: From React to Angular* offers a detailed, hands-on guide to building modern web applications that are fast, scalable, and secure. By mastering these frameworks, you'll be equipped to tackle any web development challenge and stay at the forefront of the ever-changing landscape of web technologies.

Whether you're building a personal project or working on an enterprise-level application, the skills and knowledge you gain from this book will serve as a solid foundation for your future web development career. Let's dive in and explore the power of **React**, **Angular**, and **Vue.js**, and start building modern web apps that users love!

CHAPTER 1

GETTING STARTED WITH SWIFT

Welcome to the exciting world of iOS development! In this chapter, you'll take your first steps toward becoming proficient in Swift, the programming language used to build iOS apps. Whether you're new to programming or have some experience, this chapter is designed to get you up and running with everything you need to start coding in Swift.

Installing Xcode and Setting Up Your Environment

Before you can start writing Swift code, you need to set up your development environment. Xcode is the official Integrated Development Environment (IDE) for macOS and is the go-to tool for iOS app development. Let's walk through the process of installing Xcode:

1. **Install Xcode**
   o Open the **Mac App Store** on your Mac.
   o In the search bar, type **Xcode**.
   o Click on the **Install** button. Xcode is a large file (over 10 GB), so this might take some time depending on your internet speed.

13

o   Once installed, you can open Xcode from your Applications folder.

2. **Xcode Setup**

o   Upon opening Xcode for the first time, you may be prompted to install additional components (like command-line tools) necessary for development. Simply follow the on-screen instructions to complete the setup.

3. **Creating a New Project**

o   After installing Xcode, it's time to create your first project:

- Open Xcode.
- Select **Create a new Xcode project** from the welcome screen.
- Choose a **Single View App** template, which is a simple starting point for an iOS application.
- Name your project (e.g., "HelloWorld") and choose a location to save it.
- Select **Swift** as the programming language for the project.

Now you're all set up and ready to start coding!

Understanding Swift's Basic Syntax

Swift is a powerful and expressive language, but it's also designed to be easy to learn. Below are some of the basic building blocks of Swift:

1. **Comments**
   - Comments are a way to annotate your code with notes. Swift uses both single-line (//) and multi-line (/* */) comments.

   swift

   ```
   // This is a single-line comment
   /* This is
      a multi-line
      comment */
   ```

2. **Variables and Constants**
   - Variables are values that can change, while constants are values that remain the same throughout the program.
   - In Swift, variables are declared using var and constants using let.

   swift

   ```
   var name = "John"   // Variable (can change)
   ```

15

```
let age = 30          // Constant (cannot
change)
```

3. Statements and Expressions

- ○ A statement is a line of code that performs an action. For example, declaring a variable is a statement.
- ○ An expression is a combination of values, variables, and operators that Swift can evaluate to produce a value.

```
swift
```

```
let sum = 5 + 3    // Expression (evaluates
to 8)
```

4. Semicolons

- ○ Swift does not require semicolons at the end of statements, unlike languages like Java or C.
- ○ However, semicolons are allowed if you want to write multiple statements on a single line.

```
swift
```

```
var a = 5; var b = 10  // This is valid,
but not recommended.
```

16

Writing Your First Swift Program: "Hello, World!"

Let's write your first program in Swift! This is a simple program that will display the text "Hello, World!" on the screen. Here's how you can do it:

1. Open the `ViewController.swift` file in your project.
2. Inside the `viewDidLoad()` method, write the following Swift code:

```swift
override func viewDidLoad() {
    super.viewDidLoad()

    print("Hello, World!")
}
```

3. To run the program:
   - Click the **play button** in the top-left corner of Xcode to build and run the app.
   - The app will launch in the iOS Simulator (a tool that simulates an iPhone or iPad).
   - You will see "Hello, World!" printed in the debug console at the bottom of Xcode.

This simple program demonstrates how to display output to the console, a vital first step in understanding how Swift works.

Overview of Variables, Constants, and Data Types

Now that you've written your first program, let's dive a little deeper into the building blocks of Swift: variables, constants, and data types.

1. **Variables and Constants**

    o **Variables**: Declared using `var`, they can be changed during the program's execution.

    ```swift
    swift
    ```

    ```swift
    var name = "Alice"
    name = "Bob"    // You can change the
    value of a variable
    ```

    o **Constants**: Declared using `let`, they cannot be changed after they are assigned a value.

    ```swift
    swift
    ```

    ```swift
    let pi = 3.14159    // You cannot
    change the value of pi once assigned
    ```

2. **Data Types**

    o Swift is a **type-safe** language, meaning that every variable or constant must have a specific data type. Some basic data types in Swift include:

18

- **Int**: A whole number.

```swift
```

```swift
var age: Int = 25
```

- **Double**: A floating-point number (i.e., numbers with decimals).

```swift
```

```swift
var price: Double = 19.99
```

- **String**: A sequence of characters.

```swift
```

```swift
var greeting: String = "Hello, world!"
```

- **Bool**: A true or false value.

```swift
```

```swift
var isCompleted: Bool = false
```

o Swift can also infer the type of a variable based on the value assigned to it:

```swift
```

```
var city = "London"  // Swift infers
that city is of type String
```

3. **Type Annotations**

   o In some cases, it is helpful to explicitly declare the type of a variable or constant. You can do this using type annotations:

```swift

var temperature: Double = 72.5
let isRaining: Bool = true
```

What You Learned

By the end of this chapter, you should:

- Have successfully installed Xcode and set up your development environment.
- Be familiar with Swift's basic syntax, including variables, constants, and data types.
- Understand how to write and run your first Swift program, "Hello, World!"
- Be comfortable with Swift's basic control structures, like variables, constants, and type annotations.

This chapter is your introduction to the world of Swift and iOS development. As you move forward, you'll start applying these basic concepts to more complex projects, slowly building your expertise in Swift and iOS app development.

Are you ready to continue?

CHAPTER 2

VARIABLES, CONSTANTS, AND DATA TYPES

In this chapter, we'll dive deeper into **variables**, **constants**, and **data types** in Swift. Understanding these fundamental concepts is crucial for writing clean and efficient Swift code. These building blocks will allow you to handle various forms of data within your applications, which is essential for building interactive iOS apps.

Deep Dive into Swift's Variable Declaration

In Swift, variables are used to store data that can change over time. Variables are declared using the `var` keyword, followed by the variable name, and then the value or data you want to store.

Here's the basic syntax for declaring a variable:

```swift
```

```swift
var variableName = value
```

For example, let's declare a variable to store a person's name:

```swift
```

```
var name = "John"
```

In this case, Swift will automatically infer the type of the variable based on the assigned value. This process is called **type inference** (which we'll discuss in more detail later). Since the value is a string, Swift infers that name is of type String.

Modifying Variables

Since a variable is mutable (its value can be changed), you can update its value at any time during the program:

```
swift
```

```
name = "Alice"   // Changing the value of the variable
```

Now, name will hold the string "Alice" instead of "John".

Example:

Here's a practical example where we declare a variable to store an age and then modify it:

```
swift
```

```
var age = 25
age = 26  // Updating the age value
```

Understanding Constants

Unlike variables, **constants** are values that cannot be changed once they are set. In Swift, constants are declared using the `let` keyword. Constants are used when you have a value that should not be modified throughout the program.

Here's the syntax for declaring a constant:

```swift

let constantName = value
```

For example:

```swift

let pi = 3.14159
```

Once declared, you cannot change the value of `pi`:

```swift

// This will result in an error:
pi = 3.14   // Cannot assign to value: 'pi' is a
'let' constant
```

Why Use Constants?

Constants help in protecting values that should remain fixed, improving the reliability and readability of your code. For instance, values like mathematical constants, maximum allowed user age, or application version numbers should be stored as constants.

Understanding Types: String, Int, Double, and Bool

In Swift, every piece of data has a specific **type**. The most common types you will use when building iOS apps are:

1. **String**

    o A `String` is used to store text. It can contain letters, numbers, and even special characters.

swift

```
let greeting = "Hello, Swift!"
var name = "Alice"
```

2. **Int**

    o An `Int` (short for **integer**) is used to store whole numbers without decimals.

swift

```
let age = 25
var year = 2025
```

3. **Double**

   o   A `Double` is used to store numbers with decimal points. It's especially useful when dealing with measurements or precise calculations.

```swift
```

```
let temperature = 72.5
var price = 19.99
```

4. **Bool**

   o   A `Bool` (short for **Boolean**) can only have two values: `true` or `false`. It's used to represent logical conditions, such as whether something is on or off.

```swift
```

```
let isComplete = true
var isRaining = false
```

Example: Practical Use of Different Types

Here's an example that combines all of these types:

```swift
```

```
let name = "John"          // String
let age = 30               // Int
let height = 5.9           // Double
let isStudent = true       // Bool
```

In this example:

- name holds a string (text).

- age holds an integer (whole number).

- height holds a double (decimal number).

- isStudent holds a boolean (true or false value).

Type Inference and Type Safety in Swift

1. **Type Inference**

    o Swift is a **type-safe** language, which means the type of a variable is checked at compile time. Swift automatically infers the type of a variable based on the value you assign to it. This feature is called **type inference**.

    For instance, if you assign a string to a variable, Swift will automatically treat it as a string:

```
swift
```

27

```
var city = "Paris"  // Swift infers that
city is of type String
```

Similarly, if you assign a number, Swift infers the appropriate type (in this case, `Int`):

```
swift
```

```
var age = 25  // Swift infers that age is
of type Int
```

Even if you don't explicitly declare the type, Swift will make an educated guess. However, there are times when you might want to specify the type explicitly, especially in more complex applications, to ensure clarity and avoid any potential mistakes.

```
swift
```

```
var population: Int = 1000000  // Explicit
type declaration
```

2. **Type Safety**
   o **Type safety** ensures that variables are always used in a way that matches their type. For example, you cannot assign a string to a variable that is meant to hold an integer, like this:

```
swift
```

28

```
var number: Int = 10
number = "Hello"  // Error: Cannot assign
a String to an Int
```

This type safety prevents errors and ensures your code behaves as expected.

Practical Examples: Using Data Types in Simple Apps

Let's create a simple example that uses variables and constants to calculate the price of an item after applying a discount. We'll use a combination of Int, Double, and String types.

```swift
// Constants
let itemName = "Laptop"
let originalPrice: Double = 999.99

// Variables
var discount: Double = 15.0 // Percentage
discount
var finalPrice: Double

// Calculation
finalPrice = originalPrice - (originalPrice *
discount / 100)
```

```
// Output
print("The final price of the \(itemName) after
a \(discount)% discount is $\(finalPrice)")
```

Explanation:

- `itemName` is a constant because the name of the item won't change.
- `originalPrice` is a constant, as we're assuming the original price is fixed for now.
- `discount` is a variable because the discount might change, so it's user-modifiable.
- `finalPrice` is a variable that will hold the computed final price after applying the discount.

The output might look like this:

```
swift
```

```
The final price of the Laptop after a 15.0%
discount is $849.99
```

Summary

In this chapter, we covered the following key topics:

- **Variables and Constants**: Understanding when to use `var` and `let` for mutable and immutable data.
- **Common Data Types**: `String`, `Int`, `Double`, and `Bool` — how to declare and use them in your code.
- **Type Inference and Safety**: How Swift automatically determines the type of a variable and ensures that you don't misuse data types.
- **Practical Example**: A simple discount calculation app that uses multiple data types.

Understanding these concepts will serve as the foundation for everything you build with Swift. In the next chapter, we will look at control flow in Swift, allowing you to create more dynamic apps.

CHAPTER 3

CONTROL FLOW AND LOOPS

In this chapter, we will explore how to control the flow of your program using conditional statements and loops. These are essential tools for making decisions in your code and repeating tasks. By the end of this chapter, you will be able to create dynamic programs that respond to different conditions and perform repetitive tasks efficiently.

Understanding if/else Statements

The **if/else** statement is one of the most fundamental control structures in Swift. It allows you to execute certain code only if a condition is true, and optionally execute another block of code if the condition is false.

Basic Syntax:

swift

```
if condition {
    // Code to execute if the condition is true
} else {
    // Code to execute if the condition is false
}
```

Example:

Let's say you want to check if a user is eligible to vote based on their age:

swift

```
let age = 18

if age >= 18 {
    print("You are eligible to vote.")
} else {
    print("You are not eligible to vote.")
}
```

In this case, since `age` is 18, the program will print `"You are eligible to vote."`.

More Complex Conditions:

You can also combine multiple conditions using `&&` (AND) and `||` (OR) operators.

- **AND (`&&`)**: Both conditions must be true for the block to execute.
- **OR (`||`)**: Only one of the conditions needs to be true for the block to execute.

swift

```
let age = 25
let hasID = true

if age >= 18 && hasID {
    print("You can buy alcohol.")
} else {
    print("You cannot buy alcohol.")
}
```

In this example, both conditions must be true for the message to say "You can buy alcohol."

Using Switch Statements for Control Flow

The **switch** statement is another powerful control structure in Swift. It's ideal for comparing a variable to a list of possible values, and it is especially useful when you have multiple conditions to check.

Basic Syntax:
swift

```
switch variable {
case value1:
    // Code to execute if variable equals value1
case value2:
    // Code to execute if variable equals value2
```

```
default:
    // Code to execute if variable doesn't match
any cases
}
```

Example:

Let's say we want to determine the day of the week based on a number input:

```swift
let dayNumber = 3

switch dayNumber {
case 1:
    print("Monday")
case 2:
    print("Tuesday")
case 3:
    print("Wednesday")
case 4:
    print("Thursday")
case 5:
    print("Friday")
case 6:
    print("Saturday")
case 7:
    print("Sunday")
default:
```

```
    print("Invalid day number")
}
```

In this case, since `dayNumber` is 3, the program will print "Wednesday". The `default` case handles any value that doesn't match the other cases, ensuring that the program doesn't break unexpectedly.

Switch with Ranges:

You can also use **ranges** in switch statements to check if a value falls within a certain range.

```swift
swift

let score = 85

switch score {
case 0..<50:
    print("Fail")
case 50..<75:
    print("Pass")
case 75..<90:
    print("Good")
case 90...100:
    print("Excellent")
default:
    print("Invalid score")
}
```

In this example, `score` falls in the range `75..<90`, so the program will print `"Good"`.

Mastering Loops: for-in, while, repeat-while

Loops are used to repeat a block of code multiple times. Swift offers three types of loops: **for-in, while**, and **repeat-while**. Each is useful in different situations.

for-in Loop

The `for-in` loop is commonly used to iterate over collections, such as arrays, dictionaries, and ranges.

Basic Syntax:
swift

```
for item in collection {
    // Code to execute for each item in the
collection
}
```
Example:

Let's iterate over a list of names and print each one:

swift

```
let names = ["Alice", "Bob", "Charlie", "David"]
```

```
for name in names {
    print(name)
}
```

The program will print each name in the list:

```
nginx
```

```
Alice
Bob
Charlie
David
```
Range-based for-in Loop:

You can also use `for-in` with ranges to repeat a task a set number of times.

```
swift
```

```
for i in 1...5 {
    print("Iteration \(i)")
}
```

This will print:

```
nginx
```

```
Iteration 1
Iteration 2
```

Iteration 3

Iteration 4

Iteration 5

while Loop

The `while` loop will continue executing as long as a condition remains true.

Basic Syntax:

swift

```
while condition {
    // Code to execute while the condition is
true
}
```

Example:

Let's print numbers from 1 to 5 using a `while` loop:

swift

```
var counter = 1

while counter <= 5 {
    print(counter)
    counter += 1
}
```

The program will print:

```
1
2
3
4
5
```

repeat-while Loop

The `repeat-while` loop is similar to the `while` loop, but it guarantees that the code will run at least once, even if the condition is false at the start.

Basic Syntax:

swift

```
repeat {
    // Code to execute at least once
} while condition
```

Example:

Let's print numbers from 1 to 5 using a `repeat-while` loop:

swift

```
var counter = 1

repeat {
    print(counter)
    counter += 1
```

```
} while counter <= 5
```

The output will be:

```
1
2
3
4
5
```

Real-world Example: A Basic Number-Guessing Game

Now that we understand control flow and loops, let's apply what we've learned in a fun real-world example: a simple number-guessing game.

In this game, the program will pick a random number between 1 and 100, and the user will have to guess it. The program will give feedback on whether the guess is too high, too low, or correct.

```swift
import Foundation

// Generate a random number between 1 and 100
let randomNumber = Int.random(in: 1...100)

var guessedNumber = 0
```

```
var attempts = 0

print("Welcome to the Number Guessing Game!")
print("Try to guess the number between 1 and
100.")

while guessedNumber != randomNumber {
    // Ask the user for a guess
    print("Enter your guess: ", terminator: "")
    if let userInput = readLine(), let guess =
Int(userInput) {
        guessedNumber = guess
        attempts += 1

        if guessedNumber < randomNumber {
            print("Too low! Try again.")
        } else if guessedNumber > randomNumber {
            print("Too high! Try again.")
        } else {
            print("Correct! You guessed the
number in \(attempts) attempts.")
        }
    } else {
        print("Please enter a valid number.")
    }
}
```

How it Works:

- The program generates a random number between 1 and 100 using the `random(in:)` function.
- It then enters a `while` loop, where the user is prompted to enter a guess.
- If the guess is too low, the program prints "Too low! Try again."
- If the guess is too high, the program prints "Too high! Try again."
- When the guess is correct, the program prints "Correct!" and tells the user how many attempts it took.

Summary

In this chapter, we learned:

- **if/else statements**: Used for making simple decisions in code.
- **switch statements**: A more powerful alternative to `if/else` for comparing values against multiple conditions.
- **Loops**: Including `for-in`, `while`, and `repeat-while` loops for repeating code multiple times based on conditions.

- **Real-world Example**: A number-guessing game that uses loops, conditionals, and user input to create an interactive experience.

These concepts are essential for writing dynamic, interactive apps. In the next chapter, we will dive into functions in Swift, one of the most powerful features for organizing and structuring your code.

CHAPTER 4

FUNCTIONS IN SWIFT

Functions are one of the core building blocks of Swift programming. They allow you to group a set of instructions together, making your code more modular, reusable, and organized. In this chapter, we'll explore how to create and call functions, work with parameters and return values, and understand closures—another important concept in Swift. We'll also see some practical examples of how functions are used in app navigation and other iOS development tasks.

Creating and Calling Functions

A function is a block of code that performs a specific task. Functions in Swift are defined using the `func` keyword, followed by the function name, parameters (optional), and a body that contains the code to be executed.

Basic Function Syntax:

```swift

func functionName() {
    // Code to execute
}
```

Let's define a simple function that prints a greeting:

swift

```
func sayHello() {
    print("Hello, Swift!")
}
```

You can **call** a function by using its name followed by parentheses:

swift

```
sayHello()  // This will print "Hello, Swift!"
```
Example:

Here's another example where we define a function that takes two numbers and prints their sum:

swift

```
func addNumbers(a: Int, b: Int) {
    let sum = a + b
    print("The sum is \(sum)")
}

addNumbers(a: 5, b: 3)  // This will print "The
sum is 8"
```

Function Parameters and Return Values

Functions can accept **parameters**, which are values passed into the function to modify its behavior. Additionally, functions can return a value after performing a task. This return value can be used elsewhere in your code.

Function Parameters

Parameters are defined within the parentheses following the function name. Each parameter consists of a **name** and a **type**. Multiple parameters are separated by commas.

```swift
swift

func greetUser(name: String, age: Int) {
    print("Hello, \(name)! You are \(age) years old.")
}
```

To call this function, you need to provide the arguments that match the parameter types:

```swift
swift

greetUser(name: "Alice", age: 25)   // Prints: "Hello, Alice! You are 25 years old."
```

Function Return Values

A function can also return a value using the **return** keyword. The return type must be specified after the parameter list.

```swift
```

```swift
func multiplyNumbers(a: Int, b: Int) -> Int {
    return a * b
}


let result = multiplyNumbers(a: 5, b: 4)
print("The result is \(result)")  // Prints: "The
result is 20"
```

In this example, the `multiplyNumbers` function takes two integers, multiplies them, and returns the product as an `Int`.

Return Type and Void Functions

If a function does not need to return a value, you can use **Void** as the return type (or simply omit the return type). Functions that do not return a value are commonly used for actions that perform tasks, like updating the user interface.

```swift
```

```swift
func printGreeting(name: String) {
    print("Hello, \(name)!")
```

```
}
```

In this case, `printGreeting` does not return anything, it simply performs an action (printing to the console).

Using Closures and Their Applications in iOS Development

Closures in Swift are self-contained blocks of functionality that can be passed around and used in your code. Closures are similar to functions, but they can capture and store references to variables and constants from the surrounding context in which they were created. This feature is known as **capturing values**.

Basic Closure Syntax:

A closure is defined with the following syntax:

```swift
{ (parameters) -> returnType in
    // code to execute
}
```

Here's an example of a simple closure that takes two integers and returns their sum:

```swift
```

```
let addClosure: (Int, Int) -> Int = { (a, b) in
    return a + b
}


let sum = addClosure(5, 3)
print("The sum is \(sum)")   // Prints: "The sum
is 8"
```

Shortened Closure Syntax

When using closures in Swift, you can often omit certain parts of the syntax if they can be inferred. For example, you can omit the parameter and return types when they can be inferred from the context:

```
swift
```

```
let multiplyClosure = { (a: Int, b: Int) in
    return a * b
}
```

This is functionally identical to the previous example but uses Swift's shorthand for closures.

Closures in iOS Development

Closures are widely used in iOS development, especially for tasks like handling user input, making network requests, and managing asynchronous tasks. For example, closures are used with

50

`UIAction` events, animations, and networking operations like **URLSession**.

Example: Using a Closure for Button Actions

Let's look at how closures can be used in iOS for handling button taps:

```swift
swift

let button = UIButton()

button.addAction(UIAction(handler: { action in
    print("Button tapped!")
}), for: .touchUpInside)
```

In this example, when the button is tapped, the closure is executed, printing "`Button tapped!`" to the console.

Practical Example: Functions in App Navigation

Let's combine everything we've learned about functions and closures into a real-world example: using functions and closures for app navigation.

Suppose you are building an iOS app where users can navigate between different screens (view controllers). You want to write a function that triggers navigation when a button is pressed.

Example: App Navigation Using Functions

Imagine you have two view controllers, and you want to transition from `ViewControllerA` to `ViewControllerB` when a button is pressed:

swift

```
// ViewControllerA.swift
import UIKit

class ViewControllerA: UIViewController {

    override func viewDidLoad() {
        super.viewDidLoad()

        let navigateButton = UIButton()
        navigateButton.setTitle("Go   to   Screen
B", for: .normal)
        navigateButton.addTarget(self,   action:
#selector(navigateToScreenB),              for:
.touchUpInside)

        view.addSubview(navigateButton)
    }

    @objc func navigateToScreenB() {
        let viewControllerB = ViewControllerB()
```

```
navigationController?.pushViewController(viewCo
ntrollerB, animated: true)
    }
}
```

In this example:

- The `navigateToScreenB` function is called when the button is pressed.
- This function creates an instance of `ViewControllerB` and navigates to it using `pushViewController`.

You can also pass data between the view controllers by using function parameters or closures. For instance, if you want to send data to `ViewControllerB`:

```swift
```

```
// ViewControllerA.swift
@objc func navigateToScreenB() {
    let viewControllerB = ViewControllerB(data:
"Hello from A")

navigationController?.pushViewController(viewCo
ntrollerB, animated: true)
}
```

And in `ViewControllerB`, you can define a custom initializer to accept the data:

swift

```swift
// ViewControllerB.swift
class ViewControllerB: UIViewController {
    var data: String?

    init(data: String) {
        self.data = data
        super.init(nibName: nil, bundle: nil)
    }

    required init?(coder: NSCoder) {
        fatalError("init(coder:) has not been implemented")
    }

    override func viewDidLoad() {
        super.viewDidLoad()

        print(data ?? "No data received")
    }
}
```

Summary

In this chapter, we covered:

- **Functions**: How to create and call functions, and how to pass parameters and return values.
- **Closures**: Understanding closures and how they are used in iOS development for tasks like handling button actions and managing asynchronous code.
- **App Navigation**: How functions are used to navigate between screens in an iOS app, and how you can pass data between view controllers.

Understanding functions, closures, and how they interact with app navigation is crucial for building interactive iOS apps. In the next chapter, we'll explore how to work with arrays and dictionaries to store and manage data in your apps.

CHAPTER 5

OPTIONALS IN SWIFT

In this chapter, we'll explore **optionals** in Swift. Optionals are a powerful and unique feature of Swift that helps handle the absence of a value. Understanding optionals and how to work with them is essential for writing robust, error-free Swift code. By the end of this chapter, you'll know how to safely handle optionals, unwrap them, and use them effectively in your iOS applications.

What Are Optionals?

An **optional** in Swift is a variable that can either contain a value or contain `nil` (which represents the absence of a value). Essentially, optionals are a way of saying "this value might not exist."

Declaring Optionals:

You declare an optional by adding a `?` after the type of the variable:

```swift
var name: String?  // This is an optional string
```

This means that `name` could either hold a string (like `"Alice"`) or be `nil`, representing the absence of a value.

Why Use Optionals?

Optionals are particularly useful when you deal with situations where a value might be missing. For example, user inputs or API calls can return a value, but in some cases, they might return `nil` (such as when a user does not provide their email address or a network request fails).

Unwrapping Optionals Safely with Optional Binding

To access the value inside an optional, you need to **unwrap** it. There are different ways to unwrap optionals safely in Swift, and **optional binding** is one of the most common and safest approaches.

Optional Binding Syntax:

With optional binding, you use an `if let` or `guard let` statement to check if the optional contains a value, and if it does, you can assign the unwrapped value to a new constant or variable.

```swift
if let unwrappedValue = optionalValue {
```

```
    // The value was successfully unwrapped, and
you can use unwrappedValue
    print("The        unwrapped        value        is
\(unwrappedValue)")
} else {
    // The optional was nil
    print("The value was nil.")
}
```

Example:

Here's an example where we try to unwrap an optional string:

swift

```
var name: String? = "Alice"

if let unwrappedName = name {
    print("Hello, \(unwrappedName)!")
} else {
    print("No name provided.")
}
```

Since name contains "Alice", the output will be:

```
Hello, Alice!
```

If name were nil, the output would be "No name provided."

Optional Binding with Multiple Optionals:

You can also bind multiple optionals in the same `if` `let` statement:

```swift
swift
```

```swift
var firstName: String? = "John"
var lastName: String? = "Doe"

if let first = firstName, let last = lastName {
    print("Full name is \(first) \(last)")
} else {
    print("One or both names are missing.")
}
```

If both `firstName` and `lastName` contain values, it will print the full name. If either is `nil`, it will print `"One or both names are missing."`

Optionals and Their Importance in Error Handling

Optionals play a vital role in Swift's error handling system. When something might fail (such as a network request or trying to parse a value from a string), returning an optional is a way to indicate that the operation might not produce a result.

59

For instance, when parsing a string to an integer, you can't be sure that the string will always be a valid number. Therefore, Swift provides an optional return type to represent that the operation might fail.

```swift
let validNumber = "123"
let invalidNumber = "abc"

if let number = Int(validNumber) {
    print("The number is \(number)")
} else {
    print("Invalid number.")
}

if let number = Int(invalidNumber) {
    print("The number is \(number)")
} else {
    print("Invalid number.")   // This will be printed
}
```

In this example:

- `Int(validNumber)` succeeds because "123" can be converted into an integer.
- `Int(invalidNumber)` returns `nil` because "abc" is not a valid number.

Using optionals in such situations ensures that your code remains safe and doesn't crash when unexpected input occurs.

Real-World Example: Handling Missing User Data

In real-world applications, you often need to handle user data, where some fields might be optional. Let's create a simple example where we handle user information with optionals, ensuring that the app behaves correctly when some fields are missing.

Example: User Registration Form

Imagine you have a user registration form with fields like `username`, `email`, and `phone number`. Some users might choose not to provide their email or phone number.

```swift
struct User {
    var username: String
    var email: String?
    var phoneNumber: String?
}

let user = User(username: "Alice", email: nil,
phoneNumber: "123-456-7890")
```

```
// Optional binding to safely unwrap email
if let email = user.email {
    print("User's email is \(email)")
} else {
    print("User has not provided an email.")
}


// Checking phone number
if let phone = user.phoneNumber {
    print("User's phone number is \(phone)")
} else {
    print("User    has    not    provided    a    phone
number.")
}
```

Output:

```
sql


User has not provided an email.
User's phone number is 123-456-7890
```

Explanation:

- user.email is nil, so the code inside the if let statement is not executed for the email.
- user.phoneNumber contains a value, so it is unwrapped and printed.

62

By using optionals in this way, we avoid forced unwrapping, which could cause runtime crashes if a value is missing. This approach makes the app more robust, especially when dealing with incomplete or missing user data.

Forced Unwrapping (Avoid This)

While optional binding is the safest way to deal with optionals, you can also use **forced unwrapping** to access an optional's value. However, this should be avoided unless you are certain the optional will not be `nil` because it will cause a runtime crash if the optional is `nil`.

```swift
var name: String? = "Bob"

let unwrappedName = name!  // Forced unwrapping
print(unwrappedName)
```

In this case, `name!` forces Swift to unwrap the optional. If `name` were `nil`, the app would crash with a runtime error. It's always better to use optional binding (`if let` or `guard let`) to safely handle optionals.

63

Summary

In this chapter, we covered:

- **Optionals**: What they are and how to use them to represent values that might be `nil`.
- **Optional Binding**: Using `if let` and `guard let` to safely unwrap optionals.
- **Error Handling**: The role of optionals in error handling, especially when dealing with operations that might fail (e.g., parsing strings into integers).
- **Real-World Example**: A user registration form where some fields might be missing, demonstrating how to handle optional user data safely.

Optionals are an essential feature in Swift, and understanding them will help you build safer and more reliable apps. In the next chapter, we will explore arrays and dictionaries, which are fundamental data structures used to manage collections of data.

CHAPTER 6

ARRAYS AND DICTIONARIES

In this chapter, we'll dive into two of the most important data structures in Swift: **arrays** and **dictionaries**. These structures allow you to store and manage collections of data efficiently, and they are used extensively in iOS development. We'll learn when and how to use them, how to iterate through them, and see a real-world example of storing user preferences in an app.

Understanding Arrays

An **array** in Swift is an ordered collection of values of the same type. Arrays allow you to store multiple values in a single variable, and you can access those values using an index.

Declaring and Initializing Arrays:

To declare an array, you can use the following syntax:

```swift

var arrayName: [Type] = [value1, value2, value3]
```

For example, an array of strings can be declared as:

swift

```
var fruits: [String] = ["Apple", "Banana",
"Cherry"]
```

Alternatively, Swift allows you to use **type inference**, which automatically determines the type of the array based on the values:

swift

```
var fruits = ["Apple", "Banana", "Cherry"] //
Swift infers the type [String]
```
Accessing Array Elements:

You can access an element in an array using its index. Keep in mind that arrays in Swift are **zero-indexed**, meaning the first element has an index of 0.

swift

```
let firstFruit = fruits[0] // "Apple"
print(firstFruit)
```
Modifying Arrays:

Arrays are **mutable** by default, meaning you can add, remove, or modify elements if the array is declared with var.

swift

```
fruits.append("Date")   // Adds "Date" to the end
of the array
fruits[1] = "Blueberry"   // Changes the second
element to "Blueberry"
```

You can also remove an element from the array:

```
swift
```

```
fruits.remove(at:  0)    // Removes the first
element ("Apple")
```

Understanding Dictionaries

A **dictionary** is an unordered collection of key-value pairs. Each key is unique, and it maps to a specific value. Unlike arrays, dictionaries do not maintain the order of their elements, and the keys can be any hashable type.

Declaring and Initializing Dictionaries:

To declare a dictionary, use the following syntax:

```
swift
```

```
var dictionaryName: [KeyType: ValueType] = [key1:
value1, key2: value2]
```

67

For example, a dictionary of `String` keys and `Int` values can be declared as:

swift

```
var studentGrades: [String: Int] = ["Alice": 90,
"Bob": 85, "Charlie": 92]
```

You can also use type inference:

swift

```
var studentGrades = ["Alice": 90, "Bob": 85,
"Charlie": 92]
```

Accessing Dictionary Elements:

To access a value in a dictionary, you use the key:

swift

```
let aliceGrade = studentGrades["Alice"]  // 90
print(aliceGrade ?? "No grade found")  // Prints:
90
```

If the key doesn't exist, Swift will return `nil`, so it's often a good idea to handle this possibility (e.g., using optional binding or the `??` nil-coalescing operator).

Modifying Dictionaries:

You can modify the value associated with an existing key:

```swift
swift
```

```swift
studentGrades["Alice"] = 95   // Updates Alice's grade to 95
```

To add a new key-value pair, simply assign a value to a new key:

```swift
swift
```

```swift
studentGrades["David"] = 88   // Adds a new student with grade 88
```

You can also remove a key-value pair:

```swift
swift
```

```swift
studentGrades.removeValue(forKey: "Bob")   // Removes Bob's entry
```

When and How to Use Arrays and Dictionaries in iOS Development

Arrays and dictionaries are both essential in iOS development. Here are some common use cases for each:

69

- **Arrays** are useful when you need to store ordered data, like a list of items, sequential numbers, or a collection of views in a particular order (e.g., a list of songs in a music app or a list of images in a gallery app).

- **Dictionaries** are ideal when you need to map keys to values, such as user settings, preferences, or configurations. For example, storing data where the key represents a unique identifier, and the value represents the associated data.

Use Case for Arrays:

If you are building a music app, you might store the list of songs in an array. Here's how you might represent a playlist:

swift

```swift
var playlist: [String] = ["Song 1", "Song 2", "Song 3", "Song 4"]
```

You can easily manipulate the playlist by adding or removing songs:

swift

```swift
playlist.append("Song 5")  // Add a new song
playlist.remove(at: 2)  // Remove "Song 3"
```

Use Case for Dictionaries:

If you need to store user preferences in an app, such as the user's name, preferred language, and theme preference, a dictionary is perfect:

swift

```
var userPreferences: [String: String] = [
    "name": "Alice",
    "language": "English",
    "theme": "Dark"
]
```

You can easily access or update preferences:

swift

```
userPreferences["language"] = "Spanish"     //
Change language preference
```

Iterating Through Arrays and Dictionaries

Both arrays and dictionaries can be iterated over to perform actions on each element. Swift provides efficient ways to loop through these collections.

Iterating Through an Array:

You can use a `for-in` loop to iterate over all elements in an array:

swift

```
for fruit in fruits {
    print(fruit)
}
```

If you need both the index and the element, you can use `enumerated()`:

swift

```
for (index, fruit) in fruits.enumerated() {
    print("Fruit \(index + 1): \(fruit)")
}
```

Iterating Through a Dictionary:

Similarly, you can use a `for-in` loop to iterate through key-value pairs in a dictionary:

swift

```
for (student, grade) in studentGrades {
    print("\(student) has a grade of \(grade)")
}
```

If you only need the keys or values, you can access them like this:

swift

```
// Iterate over keys
for student in studentGrades.keys {
    print(student)
}

// Iterate over values
for grade in studentGrades.values {
    print(grade)
}
```

Example: Storing User Preferences in an App

Let's build a simple example where we use both an array and a dictionary to store and manage user preferences in an iOS app. Imagine we are creating a settings screen where users can choose their preferred language and theme for the app.

swift

```
// User preferences for settings
var userSettings: [String: String] = [
    "language": "English",
    "theme": "Light"
]
```

73

```swift
// List of available themes
var availableThemes: [String] = ["Light", "Dark",
"System Default"]

// Function to change theme
func changeTheme(to newTheme: String) {
    if availableThemes.contains(newTheme) {
        userSettings["theme"] = newTheme
        print("Theme changed to \(newTheme)")
    } else {
        print("Theme not available.")
    }
}

// Change the theme to "Dark"
changeTheme(to: "Dark")
print(userSettings)    // Prints: ["language":
"English", "theme": "Dark"]
```

Explanation:

- We store the user's language and theme preferences in a dictionary (userSettings).
- We use an array (availableThemes) to store a list of possible themes.
- The changeTheme function allows the user to change the theme if it's available in the availableThemes array.
- After changing the theme, we print the updated preferences.

74

Summary

In this chapter, we covered:

- **Arrays**: Ordered collections that store values of the same type, useful for managing lists of data like songs, images, or other sequential items.
- **Dictionaries**: Unordered collections of key-value pairs, useful for mapping unique keys to associated values, such as user preferences or settings.
- **When to Use**: Arrays are perfect for ordered data, while dictionaries are best for data where each element is identified by a unique key.
- **Iterating**: Both arrays and dictionaries can be iterated over using `for-in` loops, and we learned how to access both the keys and values.
- **Real-World Example**: Storing and modifying user preferences using arrays and dictionaries.

In the next chapter, we will explore **working with optionals**, a powerful feature in Swift that allows us to handle missing or unavailable values.

CHAPTER 7

OBJECT-ORIENTED PROGRAMMING (OOP) IN SWIFT

In this chapter, we'll dive into **Object-Oriented Programming (OOP)** in Swift. OOP is a programming paradigm that is centered around objects, which can store data and have functions that act upon that data. Swift allows you to create objects using **classes** and **structs**, which are essential for creating reusable, modular, and maintainable code. We'll explore how to define properties and methods in classes, and how to use initializers and de-initializers to manage the lifecycle of objects.

Introduction to Classes and Structs

In Swift, you can define **classes** and **structs** to create custom data types. Both classes and structs allow you to store values (properties) and define functions (methods) that act on those values. However, there are important differences between them, particularly with regard to how they handle **reference types** and **value types**.

- **Classes** are **reference types**, which means when you create an instance of a class and assign it to another variable, both variables point to the same object in memory.

- **Structs** are **value types**, which means when you create an instance of a struct and assign it to another variable, a of the original struct is created.

Creating a Class:

To define a class, use the `class` keyword:

```swift
class Task {
    var title: String
    var isCompleted: Bool

    // Initializer
    init(title: String) {
        self.title = title
        self.isCompleted = false
    }

    // Method
    func markCompleted() {
        isCompleted = true
    }
}
```

Creating a Struct:

To define a struct, use the `struct` keyword:

```swift
swift

struct Task {
    var title: String
    var isCompleted: Bool

    // Method
    mutating func markCompleted() {
        isCompleted = true
    }
}
```

Notice that the `markCompleted` method is marked with `mutating` for structs. This is required because structs are value types, and calling methods that modify properties of a struct directly alters the value, which would otherwise be disallowed.

Defining Properties and Methods in Classes

Properties in classes and structs store data associated with an object, and **methods** define behavior or actions that can be performed on that data.

78

Properties:

You can define properties using the `var` keyword (for mutable properties) or `let` keyword (for constant properties).

```swift
class Task {
    var title: String  // Mutable property
    let createdAt: Date  // Constant property

    init(title: String, createdAt: Date) {
        self.title = title
        self.createdAt = createdAt
    }
}
```

In this example:

- `title` is a mutable property, and you can change its value.
- `createdAt` is a constant property, and its value cannot be changed after initialization.

Methods:

Methods are functions defined inside classes and structs that operate on the properties of an object.

```swift
swift

class Task {
    var title: String
    var isCompleted: Bool

    init(title: String) {
        self.title = title
        self.isCompleted = false
    }

    func markCompleted() {
        isCompleted = true
    }

    func displayTask() {
        print("Task:    \(title),    Completed: \(isCompleted)")
    }
}
```

In this example, `markCompleted` is a method that changes the state of the `isCompleted` property, and `displayTask` is a method that prints out the task's details.

Initializers and De-initializers

- **Initializers** are special methods in Swift classes and structs used to set up an object's properties when it is created.
- **De-initializers** are special methods used to clean up an object before it's destroyed (only available in classes).

Initializers:

An **initializer** is called when you create a new instance of a class or struct. It ensures the object is properly set up with the required properties.

swift

```
class Task {
    var title: String
    var isCompleted: Bool

    // Custom initializer
    init(title: String) {
        self.title = title
        self.isCompleted = false
    }
}
```

Here, the init method initializes a new Task object with a title, and sets isCompleted to false.

81

De-initializers:

A **de-initializer** is used to clean up any resources before an object is destroyed. It's only used in classes, and it is defined with the deinit keyword.

```swift
class Task {
    var title: String

    init(title: String) {
        self.title = title
        print("\(title) task created.")
    }

    deinit {
        print("\(title) task destroyed.")
    }
}
```

In this example, when a Task object is destroyed (when it goes out of scope or is deallocated), the deinit method is automatically called, printing a message to the console.

Example: Building a Simple App with a Class to Track Tasks

Let's use classes to build a simple task tracker. In this app, we will create a `Task` class to represent each task, and an array of tasks to store them. We will be able to mark tasks as completed and display the task list.

Step 1: Create a Task Class

swift

```swift
class Task {
    var title: String
    var isCompleted: Bool

    init(title: String) {
        self.title = title
        self.isCompleted = false
    }

    func markCompleted() {
        isCompleted = true
    }

    func displayTask() {
        let status = isCompleted ? "Completed" :
"Not completed"
        print("Task:        \(title),        Status:
\(status)")
    }
```

}

In this `Task` class:

- We have two properties: `title` (the task name) and `isCompleted` (whether the task is completed).
- The `markCompleted` method sets `isCompleted` to `true`.
- The `displayTask` method prints the task's name and its completion status.

Step 2: Create an Array of Tasks

Now, let's create an array of tasks and use methods to manipulate them.

```swift
swift

var tasks: [Task] = []

// Create some tasks
let task1 = Task(title: "Complete Swift Tutorial")
let task2 = Task(title: "Write Blog Post")
let task3 = Task(title: "Attend Team Meeting")

// Add tasks to the array
tasks.append(task1)
tasks.append(task2)
```

84

```
tasks.append(task3)

// Mark the first task as completed
task1.markCompleted()

// Display all tasks
for task in tasks {
    task.displayTask()
}
```

Step 3: Running the App

When you run the code, the tasks will be displayed, and the status of the tasks will reflect whether they are completed or not:

yaml

```
Task: Complete Swift Tutorial, Status: Completed
Task: Write Blog Post, Status: Not completed
Task: Attend Team Meeting, Status: Not completed
```

Understanding Classes vs Structs in This Example

In this chapter, we primarily focused on **classes**, which are reference types, meaning that when we pass them around, they reference the same object. If we change one instance, it will affect all references to that instance.

If you used **structs** instead of classes, each `Task` would be copied when passed around (since structs are value types). This could lead to unintended behavior when modifying data, as you would not be modifying the same instance of the `Task`.

Summary

In this chapter, we covered the following key concepts in **Object-Oriented Programming (OOP)** with Swift:

- **Classes and Structs**: The basic building blocks of OOP, and their differences (classes are reference types, structs are value types).
- **Properties and Methods**: How to define and use properties (data) and methods (functions) inside classes and structs.
- **Initializers and De-initializers**: How to set up objects when they are created, and how to clean up before they are destroyed (only in classes).
- **Real-World Example**: We built a simple task tracker app using a class to represent tasks, where we could mark tasks as completed and display the task list.

Understanding the principles of OOP will help you design more scalable and maintainable apps. In the next chapter, we will explore **enums**, which allow you to define a sct of related values in a type-safe way.

CHAPTER 8

WORKING WITH ENUMS

In this chapter, we'll explore **enums** in Swift, one of the most powerful and flexible features of the language. Enums are used to define a type that can have a set of related values. They are an excellent way to handle different states or conditions in your applications. We'll also look at **associated values** and **raw values**, which add even more functionality to enums. By the end of this chapter, you'll understand how to implement enums in your iOS apps and leverage them to manage various app states.

What Are Enums and When to Use Them?

An **enum** (short for **enumeration**) is a data type that defines a set of possible values, called **cases**. Each case represents one possible value of the enum. Enums are often used to represent a fixed number of related options, such as days of the week, types of user actions, or app states.

Enum Syntax:

Here's the basic syntax for defining an enum:

```swift
```

```
enum EnumName {
    case value1
    case value2
    case value3
}
```

For example, an enum representing the days of the week might look like this:

```
swift

enum Day {
    case monday
    case tuesday
    case wednesday
    case thursday
    case friday
    case saturday
    case sunday
}
```

When to Use Enums?

- When you need to define a set of related options or categories.
- When you want to ensure that only specific values are allowed (like app states, user roles, or status codes).
- When you want to make your code more readable and maintainable by grouping related values together.

89

Associated Values and Raw Values

While basic enums store a set of related cases, Swift allows you to go beyond just storing simple values. Enums can have **associated values** and **raw values** to store additional information.

Associated Values

Associated values allow you to store custom data with each case in an enum. This is useful when each case of the enum needs to carry different information. Think of it as storing extra details for each case.

Syntax with Associated Values:
swift

```
enum NetworkRequest {
    case success(data: String)
    case failure(error: String)
}
```

Here, each case can have associated values. For example, success carries a String with the response data, while failure carries a String with the error message.

Example:

swift

```
var result: NetworkRequest = .success(data: "Data
loaded successfully.")

switch result {
case .success(let data):
    print("Success: \(data)")
case .failure(let error):
    print("Failure: \(error)")
}
```

In this example:

- result is a variable of type NetworkRequest.
- The switch statement checks whether the result is .success or .failure.
- If it's .success, it extracts the data and prints it. If it's .failure, it extracts the error and prints it.

This way, you can store different types of data with each case of the enum, making your code more flexible.

Raw Values

In addition to associated values, enums in Swift can also have **raw values**. A **raw value** is a value that is assigned to each case in the enum. This value is the same type for all cases, and the enum can be initialized with that raw value.

Enum with Raw Values:
swift

```swift
enum Direction: String {
    case north = "North"
    case south = "South"
    case east = "East"
    case west = "West"
}
```

In this example, each case has a **raw value** of type `String`. You can use the raw value to initialize an enum:

swift

```swift
let direction = Direction(rawValue: "North")
print(direction)  // Optional(Direction.north)
```
Working with Raw Values:

You can also access the raw value of an enum case:

swift

```
let direction = Direction.north
print(direction.rawValue)  // "North"
```

Raw values are particularly useful when you need to map enum cases to external data (like storing enums in a database or parsing JSON where you know the value as a string or integer).

Real-World Example: Implementing Enums to Manage App States

One of the most practical uses of enums in iOS development is managing app states. In this example, we'll implement an enum to represent different app states such as loading, success, and failure, commonly used in network requests or any situation where the app needs to track its progress.

Step 1: Define the Enum

Let's define an enum for managing app states. The states could be:

- **loading**: The app is currently loading data.
- **success**: The app successfully completed a task (e.g., fetched data).
- **failure**: The app encountered an error.

```
swift
```

```
enum AppState {
    case loading
    case success(data: String)
    case failure(error: String)
}
```

In this example, `success` and `failure` cases have associated values to store additional information.

Step 2: Use the Enum in Your App

You can use the `AppState` enum to track the state of a network request:

```
swift
```

```
var appState: AppState = .loading

func fetchData() {
    appState = .loading
    print("Loading data...")

    // Simulating network request
    let success = true  // Imagine this is the
result of a network call

    if success {
```

```
        appState = .success(data: "Data loaded
successfully.")
        print("Data loaded successfully.")
    } else {
        appState = .failure(error: "Failed to
load data.")
        print("Error: Failed to load data.")
    }
}
```

Step 3: Handle the App State

You can use a `switch` statement to handle the different app states:

```
swift
```

```
switch appState {
case .loading:
    print("App is loading data...")
case .success(let data):
    print("App succeeded with data: \(data)")
case .failure(let error):
    print("App failed with error: \(error)")
}
```

This `switch` statement will execute different code based on the current app state. If the app is in the `loading` state, it will print "App is loading data...". If the app is in the `success` state, it will print the success message with the data. If it's in the `failure` state, it will print the error message.

95

Step 4: Simulate Changing States

Now, let's simulate the `fetchData` function call to see how the state changes:

```swift
swift


fetchData()  // Simulates loading data
switch appState {
case .loading:
    print("Still loading...")
case .success(let data):
    print("Success: \(data)")
case .failure(let error):
    print("Error: \(error)")
}
```

If `success` is set to `true`, the state will change to `.success`, and it will print the success message with the data. If `success` is `false`, it will print an error message.

Summary

In this chapter, we explored the following concepts:

- **Enums**: A way to define a set of related values that are type-safe and can be used to represent different states or categories.
- **Associated Values**: Allows you to store additional data with each case in an enum.
- **Raw Values**: Allows you to assign a constant value (such as a string or integer) to each enum case, making it easier to work with external data like JSON or databases.
- **Real-World Example**: We implemented an `AppState` enum to manage app states, such as loading, success, and failure, and showed how to use enums to control the flow of your app.

Enums are extremely useful for making your code more readable, maintainable, and type-safe. In the next chapter, we'll look at **error handling** in Swift, which is another crucial aspect of building robust iOS applications.

CHAPTER 9

ERROR HANDLING IN SWIFT

Error handling is a critical aspect of building robust iOS applications. In this chapter, we'll explore how to handle errors in Swift using the built-in error-handling mechanisms. By understanding how to throw, catch, and propagate errors, you can ensure your app behaves predictably even when things go wrong. We'll also look at practical examples, such as handling network requests and managing potential errors.

Understanding Error Types and Throwing Errors

In Swift, **errors** are represented by types that conform to the `Error` protocol. This allows you to define custom error types and handle them in a type-safe way. There are two main ways to define errors in Swift:

1. **Predefined Error Types**: Swift has a built-in `Error` protocol that can be used for error types. For simple use cases, you can use basic error types provided by the system.

2. **Custom Error Types**: You can create your own error types to represent specific failures in your application.

Defining a Custom Error Type

A custom error type in Swift is typically an enum that conforms to the `Error` protocol:

```swift
enum NetworkError: Error {
    case badURL
    case noConnection
    case serverError
    case timeout
}
```

Here, we've defined an enum called `NetworkError` with different cases to represent various types of errors that might occur during a network operation, such as a bad URL, no connection, or server errors.

Throwing Errors

You can **throw** an error using the `throw` keyword inside a function. The function that throws an error must be marked with the `throws` keyword.

```swift
func fetchData(from url: String) throws -> String
{
```

```
if url.isEmpty {
    throw NetworkError.badURL
}
// Simulate a successful network request
return "Data from \(url)"
}
```

In this example, if the `url` is empty, the function throws a `NetworkError.badURL` error. The `fetchData` function is marked with `throws` because it might throw an error during execution.

Using try, catch, and do-catch Blocks

Once you have a function that throws an error, you need to **catch** the error and handle it appropriately. Swift provides `try`, `catch`, and `do-catch` blocks for this purpose.

try

You use `try` to call a function that can throw an error:

swift

```
do {
    let data = try fetchData(from:
"https://api.example.com")
    print(data)
```

```
} catch {
    print("Error: \(error)")
}
```

In this code:

- The `try` keyword is used to call the `fetchData` function.
- If an error is thrown, it will be caught by the `catch` block, and we print the error message.

do-catch Blocks

The `do-catch` block is used to wrap code that might throw an error. It tries to execute the code within the `do` block and catches any errors in the `catch` block.

```swift
do {
    let data = try fetchData(from: "https://api.example.com")
    print("Fetched data: \(data)")
} catch let error as NetworkError {
    switch error {
    case .badURL:
        print("The URL is invalid.")
    case .noConnection:
        print("No network connection.")
    case .serverError:
```

```
        print("Server error occurred.")
    case .timeout:
        print("Request timed out.")
    }
} catch {
    print("An     unexpected     error     occurred:
\(error)")
}
```

Here:

- The do block contains the code that may throw an error.
- If the error is a NetworkError, we handle it using a switch statement in the catch block.
- If the error is not of type NetworkError, we fall back to the general catch block.

Try? and Try!

- **try?**: If you use try?, the error is converted into an optional value. If the function succeeds, the result is wrapped in an optional; if the function throws an error, the result will be nil.

swift

```
let     result     =     try?     fetchData(from:
"https://api.example.com")
```

In this case, if `fetchData` throws an error, `result` will be `nil`.

- **try!**: If you use `try!`, Swift assumes the function will not throw an error. If the function does throw an error, your app will crash.

swift

```
let    result    =    try!    fetchData(from:
"https://api.example.com")
```

Use `try!` only when you are certain the function will succeed and no errors will be thrown.

Propagating Errors and Handling Them Gracefully

In Swift, you can **propagate** errors from one function to another. If a function calls another function that throws an error, it can choose to handle the error or propagate it further up the call stack.

Propagating Errors

To propagate an error to the calling function, you use `throws` in the function signature.

swift

```
func processRequest() throws {
```

```
    let    data    =    try    fetchData(from:
"https://api.example.com")
    print("Data: \(data)")
}


do {
    try processRequest()
} catch {
    print("Error occurred: \(error)")
}
```

In this example:

- The `processRequest` function calls `fetchData`, which can throw an error.
- The error is propagated to the `do-catch` block, where it is caught and handled.

Gracefully Handling Errors

Error handling is not just about catching errors but also about ensuring your app can recover gracefully when an error occurs. Here are some tips for handling errors gracefully:

- Provide **meaningful feedback** to the user, such as showing an alert or a friendly error message when a network request fails.

- **Retry failed operations**, like attempting a network request again after a timeout or retrying a database operation.
- Use **default values** or fallback mechanisms, like using cached data if a network request fails.

Example: Handling Network Requests and Errors in iOS Apps

Let's implement a more complete example of handling network requests and errors in an iOS app. We'll simulate a network request that might fail, and then handle the error appropriately.

Step 1: Define the NetworkError Enum

swift

```
enum NetworkError: Error {
    case badURL
    case noConnection
    case serverError
    case timeout
}
```

Step 2: Simulate a Network Request Function

swift

```
func fetchData(from url: String) throws -> String
{
    if url.isEmpty {
```

```swift
        throw NetworkError.badURL
    }


    // Simulate a failure
    let success = false
    if !success {
        throw NetworkError.noConnection
    }


    // Simulate a successful request
    return "Data from \(url)"
}
```

Step 3: Handle Errors Using do-catch

swift

```swift
func loadData() {
    let url = "https://api.example.com"


    do {
        let data = try fetchData(from: url)
        print("Successfully    fetched    data:
\(data)")
    } catch let error as NetworkError {
        switch error {
        case .badURL:
            print("Error: Invalid URL.")
        case .noConnection:
            print("Error:        No        network
connection.")
```

```
    case .serverError:
        print("Error:     Server     error
occurred.")
    case .timeout:
        print("Error: Request timed out.")
    }
  } catch {
    print("An  unexpected  error  occurred:
\(error)")
  }
}
```

In this example:

- The `fetchData` function simulates a network request that might fail.
- The `loadData` function handles errors using a `do-catch` block.
- If the error is a `NetworkError`, it's handled specifically by type. Otherwise, a generic error message is shown.

Summary

In this chapter, we covered:

- **Error Types**: How to define custom error types and throw errors.

- **try, catch, and do-catch**: How to use `try` to call functions that throw errors and `catch` to handle them.
- **Propagating Errors**: How to propagate errors from one function to another and handle them gracefully.
- **Example**: We built an example to simulate a network request and handle different types of network-related errors.

Proper error handling is crucial for building reliable and user-friendly apps. In the next chapter, we will explore **working with closures**, which are essential for managing asynchronous tasks and callbacks in Swift.

CHAPTER 10

CLOSURES IN SWIFT

Closures are one of the most powerful features in Swift. They are self-contained blocks of functionality that can be passed around and used in your code. Closures are similar to functions, but they can capture and store references to variables and constants from the surrounding context in which they were created. This feature is called **capturing values**, and it makes closures very useful in situations like asynchronous operations, event handling, and callbacks in iOS development.

In this chapter, we'll cover:

1. **Understanding closures and their syntax**
2. **Capturing values and memory management with closures**
3. **Using closures with callbacks in iOS**
4. **Real-world example: Implementing closures in button actions**

Understanding Closures and Their Syntax

A **closure** in Swift is a block of code that can be passed around and executed later. Swift closures can capture and store references to variables and constants from the surrounding context in which they were defined. Closures are often used as callbacks in asynchronous tasks, and they can be passed as arguments to functions.

Basic Closure Syntax:

Here's the syntax for a simple closure in Swift:

```swift
{ (parameters) -> returnType in
    // code to execute
}
```

Let's break it down:

- **parameters**: The input values to the closure (optional).
- **returnType**: The return type of the closure (optional).
- **in**: This keyword separates the closure's parameters and return type from its body.
- The **body** of the closure contains the code to be executed.

Example:

Let's create a closure that takes two integers and returns their sum:

```swift
```

```
let addNumbers = { (a: Int, b: Int) -> Int in
    return a + b
}
```

You can then call the closure just like a function:

```
swift
```

```
let result = addNumbers(3, 5)
print(result)   // Prints: 8
```

This closure adds two integers and returns the result.

Shortened Closure Syntax:

In many cases, you can omit parts of the closure syntax if Swift can infer the types. For example:

```
swift
```

```
let addNumbers: (Int, Int) -> Int = { a, b in
    return a + b
}
```

Swift automatically infers that addNumbers is a closure that takes two integers and returns an integer.

Capturing Values and Memory Management with Closures

Closures can capture and store references to variables and constants from the surrounding context in which they are created. This feature is known as **capturing values**, and it's one of the main reasons closures are so powerful.

Capturing Values:

When a closure is created, it can capture variables from the surrounding context. Here's an example:

swift

```
func makeIncrementer(incrementAmount: Int) -> ()
-> Int {
    var total = 0
    let incrementer: () -> Int = {
        total += incrementAmount
        return total
    }
    return incrementer
}

let             incrementByFive             =
makeIncrementer(incrementAmount: 5)
print(incrementByFive())  // Prints: 5
print(incrementByFive())  // Prints: 10
```

In this example:

- The `incrementer` closure captures and stores the values of `total` and `incrementAmount` from the surrounding context.
- Each time the closure is called, it increments `total` by the captured value of `incrementAmount`.

Memory Management:

Closures that capture values can lead to strong reference cycles (retain cycles), which can cause memory leaks. Swift uses **automatic reference counting (ARC)** to manage memory. However, when closures capture self-references (such as in view controllers), it's important to break the strong reference cycle by using **weak** or **unowned** references.

Let's say you have a closure that captures a reference to `self` in a view controller. Without managing memory carefully, this could cause a strong reference cycle, preventing the view controller from being deallocated.

Using weak and unowned References:

If you use a **weak reference**, the captured reference to `self` will not prevent it from being deallocated:

swift

```
class ViewController {
    var title = "Hello"

    func fetchData(completion: @escaping () ->
Void) {
        // Using a weak reference to self to
avoid a retain cycle
        DispatchQueue.global().async    { [weak
self] in
            guard let self = self else { return
}
            print(self.title)
            completion()
        }
    }
}
```

In this case, `self` is captured weakly, meaning that if the `ViewController` is deallocated, `self` becomes `nil`, avoiding a strong reference cycle.

Using Closures with Callbacks in iOS

Closures are frequently used as **callbacks** in asynchronous operations, such as network requests or UI actions. When a task completes, a closure is executed to handle the result, allowing the app to respond to events like data loading, button presses, or background tasks.

Example: Using a Closure with a Button Action

Let's implement a closure in a button action to update the UI when a task completes. This is a common use case in iOS apps.

First, we'll define a function that simulates a network request, and then use a closure to update the UI once the request is complete.

swift

```swift
class ViewController: UIViewController {
    var loadingLabel: UILabel!

    override func viewDidLoad() {
        super.viewDidLoad()

        // Set up the loading label
        loadingLabel = UILabel()
        loadingLabel.text = "Loading..."
        view.addSubview(loadingLabel)

        // Simulate a network request
        fetchData { [weak self] result in
            self?.loadingLabel.text = result
        }
    }
```

```
// Function that simulates a network request
with a closure callback
func     fetchData(completion:     @escaping
(String) -> Void) {
    DispatchQueue.global().async {
        // Simulate a delay
        sleep(2)

        // Call the completion closure once
the task is finished
        DispatchQueue.main.async {
            completion("Data          loaded
successfully!")
        }
    }
}
```

Explanation:

- `fetchData` simulates a network request by using a `DispatchQueue` to execute code asynchronously.
- The closure parameter `completion` is called once the simulated request is finished. We pass `"Data loaded successfully!"` to the completion handler.
- Inside `viewDidLoad`, we call `fetchData` and pass a closure that updates the `loadingLabel`'s text when the task completes.

In this example, the closure serves as a callback to handle the result of the network request asynchronously.

Real-World Example: Implementing Closures in Button Actions

In this example, we'll use a closure to handle a button action in a more interactive scenario. When a button is tapped, we'll perform a task and use a closure to display a message once the task is complete.

```swift
class ViewController: UIViewController {
    var messageLabel: UILabel!

    override func viewDidLoad() {
        super.viewDidLoad()

        // Set up the label
        messageLabel = UILabel()
        messageLabel.text  =   "Waiting   for
action..."
        view.addSubview(messageLabel)

        // Set up the button
        let button = UIButton(type: .system)
        button.setTitle("Start   Task",   for:
.normal)
```

117

```swift
        button.addTarget(self,              action:
#selector(buttonTapped), for: .touchUpInside)
        view.addSubview(button)
    }


    @objc func buttonTapped() {
        // Perform some task and use closure to
handle the result
        performTask { [weak self] result in
            self?.messageLabel.text = result
        }
    }


    func    performTask(completion:    @escaping
(String) -> Void) {
        DispatchQueue.global().async {
            // Simulate some work with a delay
            sleep(3)

            // Call the closure once the task is
done
            DispatchQueue.main.async {
                completion("Task       completed
successfully!")
            }
        }
    }
}
```

Explanation:

- The `buttonTapped` method is called when the user taps the button.
- Inside `buttonTapped`, we call `performTask`, which simulates some work (like a network request or data processing).
- Once the task is complete, the closure is executed, and the message label is updated on the main thread with the result.

This approach ensures that the user interface stays responsive while the task is being performed in the background.

Summary

In this chapter, we covered the following key points about **closures** in Swift:

- **Closure Syntax**: How to define and use closures in Swift, and how to capture parameters and return values.
- **Capturing Values**: Closures can capture values from the surrounding context, allowing them to work with variables even after they go out of scope.

119

- **Memory Management**: Using weak or unowned references to avoid strong reference cycles when capturing `self` in closures.
- **Closures with Callbacks**: Using closures to handle asynchronous tasks, such as network requests, and updating the UI when tasks complete.
- **Real-World Example**: Implementing closures in button actions to perform background tasks and update the UI when finished.

Closures are an essential tool for managing asynchronous operations and callbacks in iOS development. In the next chapter, we'll explore **working with data persistence** using Core Data, which is another key aspect of building robust iOS applications.

CHAPTER 11

INTRODUCTION TO IOS DEVELOPMENT

In this chapter, we'll introduce you to the foundational concepts of **iOS development**. You'll learn how to set up your first iOS project in **Xcode**, understand the **iOS app lifecycle**, and explore the **Model-View-Controller (MVC)** design pattern. We'll also build a simple **to-do app** to put these concepts into practice.

Setting Up Your First iOS Project in Xcode

Before diving into writing code, let's set up your first iOS project using **Xcode**, which is the official Integrated Development Environment (IDE) for iOS development. Here's how you can get started:

Step 1: Install Xcode

If you haven't already installed Xcode, you can download it from the **Mac App Store**. Once installed, open Xcode and follow these steps:

Step 2: Create a New Project

1. Open **Xcode** and select **Create a new Xcode project**.

2. Choose **App** under the iOS section.

3. Select the **Swift** language and **Storyboard** for user interface design (we will use SwiftUI in later chapters).

4. Enter a **Product Name** (e.g., "TodoApp").

5. Select **Team** (if you have one, otherwise, you can choose **None**).

6. Choose **Swift** as the language and **UIKit** for the user interface (we'll cover SwiftUI in later chapters).

7. Select a **location** to save your project, then click **Create**.

Step 3: Explore the Xcode Interface

Once your project is set up, you'll see the following:

- **Project Navigator**: On the left side, you'll see all your project files.

- **Main.storyboard**: This is where you'll design your user interface (UI).

- **ViewController.swift**: This file contains the logic for your view controller.

- **Assets.xcassets**: You can manage your images and colors here.

Overview of the iOS App Lifecycle

The **iOS app lifecycle** refers to the series of events and states an app goes through from launch to termination. Understanding the app lifecycle is crucial for managing resources, handling user interactions, and optimizing performance.

Here are the key stages of the lifecycle:

1. **App Launch**: The app starts and loads its main interface.
2. **Active**: The app is running and interacting with the user.
3. **Background**: The app is running but not actively being used (e.g., playing music or updating in the background).
4. **Inactive**: The app is temporarily interrupted but is still running in the background (e.g., a phone call).
5. **Termination**: The app is terminated by the system or the user.

The `UIApplicationDelegate` protocol handles these transitions, and the `AppDelegate` class contains methods that you can use to respond to each stage of the app's lifecycle.

App Lifecycle Methods in AppDelegate:

Here are a few lifecycle methods defined in the `AppDelegate` class:

- `application(_:didFinishLaunchingWithOptions:)`: Called when the app finishes launching.
- `applicationWillResignActive(_:)`: Called when the app is about to go into the background.
- `applicationDidEnterBackground(_:)`: Called when the app enters the background.
- `applicationWillEnterForeground(_:)`: Called when the app is about to come back into the foreground.
- `applicationDidBecomeActive(_:)`: Called when the app becomes active again.
- `applicationWillTerminate(_:)`: Called when the app is about to terminate.

Understanding the Model-View-Controller (MVC) Design Pattern

The **Model-View-Controller (MVC)** design pattern is one of the most widely used patterns in iOS development. It separates the app into three distinct components:

1. **Model**: Represents the data and business logic of the app. It's responsible for managing and updating the data.
2. **View**: The user interface (UI) components that display information to the user. Views are typically what users interact with.
3. **Controller**: Acts as the intermediary between the model and the view. It updates the view when the model changes

and updates the model when the user interacts with the view.

MVC Example:

Let's break down the roles of each component with a simple example: building a **To-Do List** app.

- **Model**: A `Task` object that represents a single to-do item.
- **View**: The interface where the tasks are displayed (a table view with a list of tasks).
- **Controller**: A `ViewController` class that manages the tasks and updates the view when necessary.

Real-World Example: Building a Basic To-Do App

In this section, we'll build a simple to-do app that demonstrates how to apply the MVC design pattern in iOS development.

Step 1: Create the Model

Start by creating a `Task` model that will represent a single task in our to-do list:

```swift
swift

class Task {
```

```
var title: String
var isCompleted: Bool

init(title: String) {
    self.title = title
    self.isCompleted = false
}

func toggleCompletion() {
    isCompleted = !isCompleted
}
}
```

- **Task class**: Represents a task with a `title` and `isCompleted` status.
- The `toggleCompletion()` method changes the completion status of the task.

Step 2: Create the View (User Interface)

In `Main.storyboard`, design a simple interface that displays the list of tasks:

1. Drag a **UITableView** to the view controller.
2. Add a **UITableViewCell** to the table view to display each task.
3. Add a **UIButton** below the table view to allow users to add a new task.

Step 3: Create the Controller

In the `ViewController.swift` file, create a `ViewController` class to manage the tasks and handle user interactions.

```swift
import UIKit

class ViewController: UIViewController, UITableViewDataSource {

    var tasks: [Task] = []

    @IBOutlet weak var tableView: UITableView!

    override func viewDidLoad() {
        super.viewDidLoad()

        // Initialize some sample tasks
        tasks.append(Task(title: "Buy groceries"))
        tasks.append(Task(title: "Walk the dog"))
        tasks.append(Task(title: "Finish homework"))

        tableView.dataSource = self
    }
```

```swift
// Table view data source methods
func tableView(_ tableView: UITableView,
numberOfRowsInSection section: Int) -> Int {
    return tasks.count
}


func tableView(_ tableView: UITableView,
cellForRowAt indexPath: IndexPath) ->
UITableViewCell {
    let cell =
tableView.dequeueReusableCell(withIdentifier:
"TaskCell", for: indexPath)
    let task = tasks[indexPath.row]

    // Configure the cell
    cell.textLabel?.text = task.title
    cell.accessoryType = task.isCompleted ?
.checkmark : .none

    return cell
}

// Add a new task
@IBAction func addTask() {
    let newTask = Task(title: "New Task")
    tasks.append(newTask)
    tableView.reloadData()
}
```

```
}
```

Explanation:

- **Model**: The `Task` class represents the data for each task.
- **View**: The table view (`UITableView`) displays the list of tasks.
- **Controller**: The `ViewController` class manages the tasks and updates the table view when new tasks are added.
- The `tableView(_:numberOfRowsInSection:)` method returns the number of tasks.
- The `tableView(_:cellForRowAt:)` method configures each cell to display a task's title and checkmark based on its completion status.
- The `addTask()` method adds a new task to the list and reloads the table view to reflect the changes.

Step 4: Final Touches

- You can now run the app in the iOS Simulator. You'll see a list of tasks, and when you tap the "Add Task" button, a new task is added to the list.
- You can extend the functionality by adding a way to mark tasks as completed (e.g., by tapping the cell or adding a button to toggle completion).

129

Summary

In this chapter, we covered:

- **Setting up your first iOS project**: Creating an Xcode project and navigating the development environment.
- **The iOS app lifecycle**: Understanding the key stages of an app's lifecycle, such as launch, background, and termination.
- **Model-View-Controller (MVC)**: The design pattern used to separate concerns in your iOS app: data (Model), UI (View), and business logic (Controller).
- **Building a basic to-do app**: Implementing a simple to-do app to demonstrate MVC and how to structure an app with a `Task` model, a table view for the view, and a view controller for the logic.

This foundational knowledge is essential for any iOS app you build. In the next chapter, we'll delve into **working with data persistence** using Core Data, enabling you to save user data between app sessions.

CHAPTER 12

VIEWS AND VIEW CONTROLLERS

In this chapter, we will dive into **Views** and **View Controllers**, two fundamental components in iOS app development. Views represent the visual elements on the screen, while view controllers manage the app's interface and handle user interaction. We will also explore how to use **Interface Builder** to design your user interface visually. Finally, we'll walk through an example of building a simple form app with multiple views.

Creating and Managing Views in Your App

In iOS, **views** are objects that manage the display of information. Every visible element on the screen, such as a button, label, text field, or image, is a view. Views are managed by view controllers, which handle their interaction with the app.

Basic View Types in iOS:

1. **UILabel**: Displays text.
2. **UIButton**: Represents a clickable button.
3. **UITextField**: Allows users to input text.

4. **UIImageView**: Displays images.

5. **UIStackView**: Used to arrange views in a stack (horizontal or vertical).

6. **UIScrollView**: Allows content to scroll when it doesn't fit on the screen.

Creating Views Programmatically:

While **Interface Builder** is often used to design UI elements, it's also possible to create views programmatically in code.

Here's how to create and configure a `UILabel` in Swift:

```swift
let label = UILabel()
label.frame = CGRect(x: 50, y: 100, width: 300,
height: 40)
label.text = "Hello, World!"
label.textColor = .black
view.addSubview(label)
```

This code creates a `UILabel` and adds it to the view. You specify its position, size, text, and color programmatically.

Understanding View Controllers and Their Role in iOS Apps

A **view controller** is responsible for managing the views in a screen of your app. It serves as the intermediary between the views and the data model, controlling the app's behavior and logic. View controllers handle user interaction (like button taps or text field inputs), update views, and manage transitions between different screens (views).

Lifecycle of a View Controller:

A view controller has several key lifecycle methods:

- **viewDidLoad()**: Called when the view controller's view is loaded into memory. This is where you typically set up your UI.
- **viewWillAppear()**: Called just before the view is displayed.
- **viewDidAppear()**: Called after the view has been displayed.
- **viewWillDisappear()**: Called just before the view is removed from the screen.
- **viewDidDisappear()**: Called after the view is removed from the screen.

```swift

override func viewDidLoad() {
```

133

```
    super.viewDidLoad()
    // This is where you'll set up your UI and
logic
    print("View has loaded.")
}
```

Example: Creating a View Controller

Here's how a basic `UIViewController` looks in Swift:

```swift
swift

import UIKit

class MyViewController: UIViewController {

    override func viewDidLoad() {
        super.viewDidLoad()
        // View setup goes here
        self.view.backgroundColor = .white

        let label = UILabel()
        label.text = "Welcome to my app!"
        label.frame = CGRect(x: 50, y: 100,
width: 200, height: 40)
        view.addSubview(label)
    }
}
```

In this example, `MyViewController` sets the background color of the view to white and adds a `UILabel` with some text.

Using Interface Builder to Design UI Elements

Interface Builder is a graphical tool in Xcode that allows you to design your app's user interface visually. You can drag and drop UI elements (like buttons, labels, text fields, etc.) onto the screen and set their properties.

Creating Views in Interface Builder:

1. **Open the Storyboard**: Open `Main.storyboard` in your Xcode project. This file contains your app's UI.

2. **Drag and Drop UI Elements**: From the **Object Library** (right side), drag UI components like `UILabel`, `UIButton`, and `UITextField` onto the canvas.

3. **Set Constraints**: Use **Auto Layout** to set constraints, ensuring your UI elements are positioned correctly across different screen sizes.

4. **Connect UI Elements to Code**: Control-drag from a UI element in the storyboard to your view controller code to create an **IBOutlet** (for referencing UI elements) or an **IBAction** (for handling user actions).

Example of Connecting UI Elements to Code:

Let's say you've added a `UIButton` in Interface Builder, and you want to create an action for it when tapped.

1. In Interface Builder, control-drag from the button to your `ViewController.swift` file.

2. Release the drag and select **Action** to create an IBAction method.

This will create the following code:

```swift
@IBAction func buttonTapped(_ sender: UIButton)
{
    print("Button was tapped!")
}
```

This method will be triggered when the user taps the button, and it will print "`Button was tapped!`" to the console.

Example: Building a Simple Form App with Multiple Views

Now, let's build a basic app with multiple views. In this example, we'll create a simple **form app** where users can input their name and email, and then display that information on another screen.

136

Step 1: Create the First View (Form View)

In **ViewController.swift**, create a form with two text fields and a button.

swift

```
import UIKit

class FormViewController: UIViewController {

    @IBOutlet    weak    var    nameTextField:
UITextField!
    @IBOutlet    weak    var    emailTextField:
UITextField!

    override func viewDidLoad() {
        super.viewDidLoad()
        // Additional setup if needed
    }

    @IBAction    func    submitForm(_    sender:
UIButton) {
        let  name  =  nameTextField.text  ??  "No
name"
        let  email  =  emailTextField.text  ??  "No
email"

        // Navigate to the next view controller
```

```
    performSegue(withIdentifier:
"showDetails", sender: nil)
    }


    override    func    prepare(for    segue:
UIStoryboardSegue, sender: Any?) {
        if segue.identifier == "showDetails" {
            let        destinationVC        =
segue.destination as! DetailsViewController
            destinationVC.name              =
nameTextField.text
            destinationVC.email             =
emailTextField.text
        }
    }
}
```

Here:

- `nameTextField` and `emailTextField` are connected as **IBOutlets**.
- When the user taps the submit button, the app navigates to another screen (the **DetailsViewController**), passing the entered name and email as data.

Step 2: Create the Second View (Details View)

Create a second view controller that displays the submitted information. In **DetailsViewController.swift**, add the following code:

swift

```
import UIKit

class DetailsViewController: UIViewController {

    @IBOutlet weak var nameLabel: UILabel!
    @IBOutlet weak var emailLabel: UILabel!

    var name: String?
    var email: String?

    override func viewDidLoad() {
        super.viewDidLoad()

        nameLabel.text = name
        emailLabel.text = email
    }
}
```

Here:

- `nameLabel` and `emailLabel` are **IBOutlets** connected to `UILabel` elements in the storyboard.
- The `name` and `email` properties are set from the previous view controller when the segue is performed.

Step 3: Set Up the Storyboard

1. Create two view controllers in the storyboard: one for the form and one for the details view.
2. Design the form in the first view controller with two `UITextField`s for the name and email, and a `UIButton` for submission.
3. Add labels in the second view controller to display the user's name and email.
4. Create a **segue** from the **submit button** in the form view to the details view controller. Set its identifier to `"showDetails"`.

Now, when you run the app, users can input their name and email in the form. When they tap the submit button, the app transitions to the details view and displays the submitted data.

Summary

In this chapter, we covered the following key concepts:

- **Views and View Controllers**: Views display content, and view controllers manage the behavior of views and handle user interactions.
- **Interface Builder**: A visual tool in Xcode for designing the user interface by dragging and dropping UI elements.
- **Building a Simple Form App**: A real-world example where we used multiple views to create a simple form app. We used `UITextField` for input, `UIButton` for actions, and passed data between view controllers using segues and preparation methods.

Mastering views, view controllers, and Interface Builder is essential for building interactive and user-friendly iOS applications. In the next chapter, we'll explore how to handle **navigation controllers** and manage navigation between multiple screens in a more complex app.

CHAPTER 13

AUTO LAYOUT AND CONSTRAINTS

In this chapter, we'll explore **Auto Layout** and how it is used in iOS to create responsive and adaptable user interfaces. With the vast array of iPhone and iPad screen sizes and resolutions, Auto Layout ensures that your app's user interface will look great on any device. We'll cover the basics of Auto Layout, explain how constraints work, and walk through a practical example of building a layout that works on all screen sizes.

Introduction to Auto Layout and Its Importance

Auto Layout is a system that allows you to define the relationships between user interface elements in your app. These relationships are defined using **constraints**, which describe how elements should be positioned and sized relative to each other.

Why Auto Layout Is Important:

1. **Device Variety**: With iOS, there are many different device types and screen sizes. Auto Layout ensures that your app's UI adapts to different screen sizes,

orientations, and resolutions without having to manually adjust layouts for each device.

2. **Orientation Flexibility**: Auto Layout helps in creating layouts that automatically adjust when the device orientation changes from portrait to landscape.

3. **Resolution Independence**: With Auto Layout, your layout remains flexible, even with different screen resolutions, making sure your app looks sharp and crisp on all devices.

Instead of manually setting fixed positions and sizes for elements, Auto Layout allows you to use constraints to describe the relationships between UI elements. These constraints enable the UI to adapt dynamically to different screen sizes and orientations.

Understanding Constraints for Responsive Design

A **constraint** is a rule that defines the position, size, or alignment of a UI element relative to other elements or the parent view. Constraints allow the layout to be flexible and respond to different screen sizes.

Types of Constraints:

1. **Position Constraints**:

o   Define where a view is positioned relative to other views or the parent view.

o   Example: Aligning a button to the center of the screen or pinning a label to the top edge of the parent view.

2. **Size Constraints**:

o   Define the width and height of a view, either as fixed values or relative to other views.

o   Example: Setting a view to have a width of 50% of the screen width or a fixed height of 100 points.

3. **Spacing Constraints**:

o   Define the space between two views.

o   Example: Placing a button 20 points below a label.

4. **Aspect Ratio**:

o   Defines the ratio between the width and height of a view. Useful for images or elements that need to maintain a specific ratio.

Adding Constraints in Interface Builder:

In Xcode, you can add constraints visually using **Interface Builder**:

1. Select the view or UI element you want to apply constraints to.

2. Use the **Auto Layout toolbar** (located at the bottom-right corner of Interface Builder) to add constraints for positioning, spacing, and size.

3. Xcode will automatically calculate the best position and size for your UI elements based on the constraints you add.

Constraint Priorities:

Each constraint has a **priority**, which tells Auto Layout how to handle conflicts if multiple constraints are in place. The default priority is 1000, which means the constraint is required. Lower priority constraints (e.g., 750) are used when Auto Layout has to resolve conflicts or adjust layouts.

Practical Example: Building a Layout That Works on All Screen Sizes

Let's build a simple layout that works across various screen sizes, using **Auto Layout** and constraints. In this example, we'll create a basic form with a **UILabel**, **UITextField**, and **UIButton**, ensuring the layout adapts to any screen size.

Step 1: Create the UI Elements

In **Main.storyboard**:

1. Drag a **UILabel** onto the screen. This label will display a title for the form.

2. Add a **UITextField** below the label for user input.

3. Add a **UIButton** below the text field for submitting the form.

Step 2: Add Constraints to the UI Elements

We'll use **Auto Layout** constraints to ensure that the UI elements are properly aligned and sized:

1. **Label Constraints**:
   - Pin the label to the top of the screen with a fixed margin (e.g., 50 points from the top).
   - Center the label horizontally in the parent view (the screen).

2. **Text Field Constraints**:
   - Pin the text field 20 points below the label.
   - Set the width of the text field to be equal to 80% of the parent view's width.
   - Center the text field horizontally.

3. **Button Constraints**:
   - Pin the button 20 points below the text field.
   - Set the width of the button to be equal to the text field's width.
   - Center the button horizontally in the parent view.

Step 3: Apply the Constraints in Interface Builder

1. Select the **UILabel** and click on the **Add New Constraints** button in the Auto Layout toolbar. Set the top constraint to 50 points, and the center constraint horizontally.

2. Select the **UITextField** and set its top constraint to 20 points below the label. Then set the width constraint to 80% of the parent view's width and center it horizontally.

3. Select the **UIButton** and set its top constraint to 20 points below the text field. Apply the same width constraint as the text field to maintain consistency and center it horizontally.

Step 4: Running the App on Different Screen Sizes

Now that we have applied Auto Layout constraints, the layout will adjust automatically based on the screen size. For example:

- On smaller devices like the iPhone SE, the form elements will be sized and spaced to fit the screen.
- On larger devices like the iPhone 12 or iPad, the form elements will still maintain their relative positioning and proportions.

You can test the responsiveness of the layout by using the **Simulator** in Xcode and switching between different device types and orientations.

Understanding Intrinsic Content Size and Priorities

Some UI elements, such as `UILabel`, `UITextField`, and `UIButton`, have an **intrinsic content size**, which means their size is determined by the content they display (e.g., the length of the text in a label). Auto Layout uses this intrinsic content size when calculating the layout of the view.

For example, a button will automatically adjust its width based on the text it contains, but you can set **constraints** to control its size relative to other elements.

Additionally, when using Auto Layout, it's important to understand the concept of **priorities**. If two constraints conflict (e.g., a view cannot be both 100 points wide and 200 points wide at the same time), Auto Layout will try to resolve the conflict based on the priority of the constraints.

Summary

In this chapter, we covered the following key concepts:

- **Auto Layout**: A system that allows you to define the relationships between views using constraints, ensuring that your UI adapts to different screen sizes and orientations.

- **Constraints**: Rules that define how views should be positioned and sized relative to other views or the parent view.

- **Intrinsic Content Size**: The size of a view determined by its content (e.g., text in a label or button).

- **Practical Example**: Building a simple form app with Auto Layout, where we added constraints to ensure the form adapts to different screen sizes.

Understanding Auto Layout is essential for creating flexible and responsive iOS apps. In the next chapter, we will dive deeper into **navigation controllers** and how to manage navigation between different views in your app.

Are you ready to move on to the next chapter, or would you like to revisit any of the concepts discussed?

CHAPTER 14

STORYBOARDS AND NAVIGATION CONTROLLERS

In this chapter, we will explore how to use **storyboards** and **navigation controllers** in iOS to create multi-screen apps and manage navigation between views. Storyboards are a powerful tool in Xcode for visually designing your app's user interface, and navigation controllers allow you to manage transitions between different views in your app seamlessly. We'll also walk through an example of building a simple multi-screen app with navigation.

Working with Storyboards in Xcode

A **storyboard** in Xcode is a visual representation of your app's UI. It allows you to design multiple screens (view controllers) and define the transitions between them. Storyboards simplify the process of designing the UI and managing the flow of your app. By connecting view controllers with segues, you can easily create navigation between different screens.

Creating a New View Controller in a Storyboard

To add a new view controller to your storyboard:

1. Open **Main.storyboard** in Xcode.

2. From the **Object Library**, drag and drop a **View Controller** onto the canvas.

3. You can then design the UI for this view controller by adding UI elements like labels, buttons, and text fields.

Designing UI Elements in the Storyboard

- **UILabel**: Displays static text.
- **UIButton**: Triggers actions when tapped.
- **UITextField**: Collects user input.
- **UIImageView**: Displays images.

Each of these elements can be customized with Auto Layout constraints to make the UI responsive to different screen sizes.

Using Segues to Connect View Controllers

A **segue** defines the transition from one view controller to another. You can create segues between view controllers in the storyboard by **control-dragging** from one view controller to another.

Here's how you can create a segue:

1. Control-drag from a UI element (like a button) in the first view controller to the second view controller.

2. Select the type of segue you want to create (e.g., **show** or **modal**).

3. Assign an **identifier** to the segue in the attributes inspector. This identifier will be used to reference the segue in code.

Example of a Simple Segue:

In your **ViewController.swift**, you can perform the segue programmatically when an action occurs, such as a button tap:

```swift
swift

@IBAction    func    goToNextScreen(_    sender:
UIButton) {
    performSegue(withIdentifier:
"showDetailScreen", sender: nil)
}
```

In this example:

- `performSegue(withIdentifier:)` triggers the segue with the identifier `showDetailScreen`.

Implementing Navigation Controllers for App Navigation

A **navigation controller** is a special type of view controller that manages a stack of view controllers and provides navigation features, such as the ability to push and pop view controllers, displaying a navigation bar, and supporting back navigation.

Navigation controllers are essential for creating apps with hierarchical navigation, where each screen (view controller) leads to another screen.

Adding a Navigation Controller

To add a navigation controller to your app:

1. In your storyboard, select the initial view controller.
2. In the **Editor** menu, select **Embed in > Navigation Controller**. This adds a navigation controller and embeds the selected view controller in it.
3. A navigation bar will automatically appear at the top of the screen, and the navigation controller will manage transitions between screens.

Pushing and Popping View Controllers

Once your app is embedded in a navigation controller, you can use **push** and **pop** methods to navigate between screens.

- **Pushing a View Controller**: This adds a new view controller to the stack.
- **Popping a View Controller**: This removes the current view controller from the stack and returns to the previous screen.

Here's an example of pushing a new view controller in your `ViewController.swift`:

swift

```
@IBAction func goToNextScreen(_ sender:
UIButton) {
    let detailViewController =
DetailViewController()

navigationController?.pushViewController(detail
ViewController, animated: true)
}
```

In this example, when the user taps a button, the app pushes a new view controller (`DetailViewController`) onto the navigation stack.

Navigation Bar Customization

The **navigation bar** at the top of the screen can be customized to display a title, buttons, and other UI elements. For example, you can set the title of a view controller's navigation bar:

swift

```
self.title = "Detail Screen"
```

Additionally, you can add a **back button** that appears when you push a new view controller:

swift

```swift
let backButton = UIBarButtonItem(title: "Back",
style: .plain, target: self, action:
#selector(backButtonTapped))
self.navigationItem.leftBarButtonItem    =
backButton
```

Example: Building a Multi-Screen App with Navigation

Let's now build a simple multi-screen app that demonstrates navigation between two screens using a navigation controller.

Step 1: Create the View Controllers

In the storyboard:

1. Add two view controllers (FirstViewController and SecondViewController).
2. Embed the first view controller in a navigation controller.
3. Create a button in FirstViewController to navigate to SecondViewController.

Step 2: Define the Segue and Button Action

1. Control-drag from the button in `FirstViewController` to `SecondViewController` to create a segue.
2. Set the segue identifier to `"showSecondViewController"`.

In `FirstViewController.swift`, create an action to perform the segue:

swift

```
@IBAction func goToSecondScreen(_ sender:
UIButton) {
    performSegue(withIdentifier:
"showSecondViewController", sender: nil)
}
```

Step 3: Set Up `SecondViewController`

In `SecondViewController.swift`, you can modify the navigation bar to show a custom title:

swift

```
class SecondViewController: UIViewController {
    override func viewDidLoad() {
        super.viewDidLoad()
        self.title = "Second Screen"
```

156

```
    }
}
```

Step 4: Run the App

Now, when you run the app:

- The first screen will have a button. When the button is tapped, the app will segue to the second screen using the navigation controller.
- The navigation bar will show a title on each screen, and you can navigate back to the first screen using the back button automatically provided by the navigation controller.

Summary

In this chapter, we covered the following concepts:

- **Storyboards**: A visual way to design your app's user interface in Xcode. You can define view controllers, layout elements, and segues between screens.
- **Navigation Controllers**: A special type of view controller used to manage a stack of view controllers and provide navigation features like a back button and navigation bar.
- **Creating Segues**: Connecting view controllers and managing navigation transitions using segues.

- **Building a Multi-Screen App**: Using a navigation controller to create a simple app with multiple screens and navigating between them using segues and programmatic navigation.

Understanding storyboards and navigation controllers is essential for building well-structured, multi-screen apps in iOS. In the next chapter, we will explore **Table Views** and how to display lists of data efficiently.

CHAPTER 15

HANDLING USER INPUT

In this chapter, we'll explore how to work with user input in iOS applications. User input is a crucial part of interactive apps, and iOS provides several UI elements like **text fields**, **buttons**, and other controls to capture user interactions. We'll also learn how to use **IBAction** and **IBOutlet** to link UI elements to your code, enabling your app to respond to user actions. Finally, we'll create a simple **calculator app** as a practical example.

Working with Text Fields, Buttons, and Other User Interface Elements

To capture and interact with user input, you'll typically use the following common UI elements:

1. **UITextField**: A UI element that allows the user to enter text, such as a name, email, or number.

2. **UIButton**: A clickable button that responds to taps. Buttons are used to trigger actions in your app.

3. **UILabel**: A UI element that displays static text, typically used to show results or labels.

4. **UISwitch**: A toggle switch to represent two states, such as on/off.

5. **UISlider**: A horizontal slider that allows the user to select a value from a continuous range.

Creating a UITextField (Text Input)

The UITextField is used to capture single-line text input from the user. It's often used for forms, search bars, and calculators.

1. Drag a **UITextField** from the Object Library onto the storyboard.
2. Set the placeholder text, which will be displayed when the text field is empty.
3. You can also set properties like **keyboard type** to specify whether the keyboard is numeric, email, or default.

Creating a UIButton (Button Input)

The UIButton is used to trigger an action when it is tapped by the user. To create a button:

1. Drag a **UIButton** from the Object Library onto the storyboard.
2. Set its title and customize its appearance (e.g., color, corner radius).
3. You can change the button's style to be **System**, **Custom**, or **Rounded** depending on the design.

Responding to User Actions with IBAction and IBOutlet

In iOS development, you use **IBOutlet** and **IBAction** to connect user interface elements to your code.

- **IBOutlet** (Interface Builder Outlet) is used to link UI elements to variables in your code. This allows you to access and modify these UI elements programmatically.
- **IBAction** (Interface Builder Action) is used to connect UI elements like buttons to methods in your code. This allows you to define actions that will occur when the user interacts with the UI element.

Creating IBOutlets and IBActions:

1. Open the **Assistant Editor** by selecting **View > Assistant Editor > Show Assistant Editor**.
2. Control-drag from a UI element (e.g., a text field or button) to your `ViewController.swift` file.
3. Choose **Outlet** to create an IBOutlet (for connecting the element to your code) or **Action** to create an IBAction (for handling user interactions).

Example:

Here's an example of how you can connect a `UITextField` and `UIButton` to your code.

161

1. **UITextField Outlet**:

```swift
swift
```

```swift
@IBOutlet   weak   var   numberTextField:
UITextField!
```

2. **UIButton Action**:

```swift
swift
```

```swift
@IBAction   func   calculateButtonTapped(_
sender: UIButton) {
    if        let       inputText       =
numberTextField.text,   let   number   =
Double(inputText) {
        print("User entered: \(number)")
    }
}
```

- The `IBOutlet` connects the `UITextField` to the `numberTextField` variable in the code, allowing you to access and manipulate the text field's value.
- The `IBAction` connects the button tap to the `calculateButtonTapped` method, which will be executed when the button is pressed.

Example: Creating a Simple Calculator App

Now, let's apply what we've learned and create a simple **calculator app** that takes two numbers from the user, performs an arithmetic operation (addition), and displays the result.

Step 1: Designing the UI in Storyboard

1. Add two **UITextField** elements for entering numbers.
2. Add a **UIButton** that will trigger the calculation.
3. Add a **UILabel** to display the result.
4. Use **Auto Layout** to position the elements on the screen so that the app is responsive on different screen sizes.

Step 2: Linking UI Elements to Code

In **ViewController.swift**, create IBOutlets for the text fields and label, and an IBAction for the button.

```swift
import UIKit

class ViewController: UIViewController {

    @IBOutlet weak var firstNumberTextField: UITextField!
    @IBOutlet weak var secondNumberTextField: UITextField!
```

```
@IBOutlet weak var resultLabel: UILabel!

override func viewDidLoad() {
    super.viewDidLoad()
    // Setup code if needed
}


@IBAction func calculateSum(_ sender:
UIButton) {
    if let firstText =
firstNumberTextField.text, let secondText =
secondNumberTextField.text,
        let firstNumber = Double(firstText),
let secondNumber = Double(secondText) {

        let sum = firstNumber + secondNumber
        resultLabel.text = "Result: \(sum)"
    } else {
        resultLabel.text = "Please enter
valid numbers"
    }
}
}
```

Explanation:

- We created **IBOutlets** to connect the text fields
  (firstNumberTextField,
  secondNumberTextField) and the label
  (resultLabel) to our code.

- The **IBAction** `calculateSum` is triggered when the user taps the "Calculate" button.
  - ○ We retrieve the text from both text fields, convert them into `Double` values, and then calculate their sum.
  - ○ If the user entered invalid input, we display an error message.

Step 3: Running the App

When you run the app:

1. Enter two numbers into the text fields.
2. Tap the "Calculate" button.
3. The result of the addition will be displayed in the label.

This simple calculator app demonstrates how to handle basic user input and perform calculations in response to user actions.

Enhancing the Calculator App

To make this app more complete, you can:

- Add additional buttons for subtraction, multiplication, and division.
- Handle edge cases such as dividing by zero.

165

- Add additional validations for empty fields or non-numeric input.

Here's how you might modify the app to handle multiple operations:

swift

```
@IBAction func calculate(_ sender: UIButton) {
    if let firstText =
firstNumberTextField.text, let secondText =
secondNumberTextField.text,
        let firstNumber = Double(firstText), let
secondNumber = Double(secondText) {

        var result: Double = 0
        switch sender.titleLabel?.text {
        case "Add":
            result = firstNumber + secondNumber
        case "Subtract":
            result = firstNumber - secondNumber
        case "Multiply":
            result = firstNumber * secondNumber
        case "Divide":
            if secondNumber != 0 {
                result = firstNumber /
secondNumber
            } else {
```

166

```
                    resultLabel.text    =    "Cannot
divide by zero"
                return
            }
        default:
            break
        }


        resultLabel.text = "Result: \(result)"
    } else {
        resultLabel.text = "Please enter valid
numbers"
    }
}
```

This modification uses a **switch** statement to handle different arithmetic operations based on the button's label.

Summary

In this chapter, we covered the following concepts:

- **UITextField**: Captures text input from the user.
- **UIButton**: Triggers actions when tapped.
- **UILabel**: Displays information or results.

- **IBOutlet and IBAction**: Used to link UI elements in Interface Builder to your code and respond to user interactions.
- **Creating a Simple Calculator App**: We built a basic calculator that takes two numbers from the user and displays the result.

Handling user input is essential for building interactive apps. By using `UITextField`, `UIButton`, and `UILabel`, you can create powerful forms and user interfaces that respond to user interactions. In the next chapter, we'll explore how to work with **table views** to display dynamic lists of data.

CHAPTER 16

WORKING WITH TABLE VIEWS

In this chapter, we will explore **table views**, one of the most commonly used UI components in iOS development. Table views are essential for displaying lists of data and are used extensively in apps to show things like contact lists, settings, and news feeds. We'll cover the basics of using **UITableView** to display lists of data, handling table view data with **arrays**, and implement a real-world example to display a list of items in a table view.

Introduction to Table Views and Their Role in iOS Apps

A **table view** is a scrollable list of rows, each of which can contain content. It's commonly used to display structured data in a single-column list format, such as:

- Lists of contacts in a phone app
- To-do items in a task manager
- News articles in a feed

Table views are highly flexible and can be customized to display various types of data, such as plain text, images, and interactive buttons.

In iOS, **UITableView** is the class responsible for creating and managing these lists. You use it to efficiently display and manage large sets of data while keeping memory usage low.

Basic Table View Components:

- **UITableView**: The main container that holds and displays the rows.
- **UITableViewCell**: Represents a single row in the table view.
- **UITableViewDataSource**: A protocol that provides the data for the table view.
- **UITableViewDelegate**: A protocol that allows you to respond to user interactions, such as selecting rows.

Using UITableView to Display Lists of Data

To display a list of data in a table view, you need to configure the table view's data source and delegate, implement required methods, and bind your data (such as an array) to the table view.

Step 1: Setting Up the UITableView

1. In **Main.storyboard**, drag a **UITableView** onto the screen.
2. Add constraints to the table view to make it resize properly across different screen sizes.

3. Create a **UITableViewCell** by dragging a **Table View Cell** inside the table view. You can customize the cell with a label, image view, etc.

4. Set the **reuse identifier** for the cell (e.g., cellIdentifier) in the attributes inspector.

Step 2: Connecting the UITableView to Your Code

1. Open the **Assistant Editor** and control-drag from the table view in the storyboard to your ViewController.swift file to create an **IBOutlet** for the table view.

swift

```
@IBOutlet weak var tableView: UITableView!
```

2. Conform your view controller to the UITableViewDataSource and UITableViewDelegate protocols:

swift

```
class ViewController: UIViewController, UITableViewDataSource, UITableViewDelegate {
    // Your code will go here
}
```

171

3. Implement the necessary data source methods to provide data to the table view:

swift

```swift
func tableView(_ tableView: UITableView,
numberOfRowsInSection section: Int) -> Int {
    return items.count
}

func tableView(_ tableView: UITableView,
cellForRowAt indexPath: IndexPath) ->
UITableViewCell {
    let cell =
tableView.dequeueReusableCell(withIdentifier:
"cellIdentifier", for: indexPath)
    cell.textLabel?.text = items[indexPath.row]
    return cell
}
```

Handling Table View Data with Arrays

To populate your table view with data, you typically use an **array** or other collection types like dictionaries or models. The UITableViewDataSource methods will return the data that the table view needs to display.

172

Step 3: Creating and Using an Array for Data

Let's create an array of strings to display a list of items in the table view.

swift

```
var items = ["Item 1", "Item 2", "Item 3", "Item 4", "Item 5"]
```

In the `tableView(_:numberOfRowsInSection:)` method, you will return the count of the `items` array to determine how many rows to display in the table view.

swift

```
func tableView(_ tableView: UITableView, numberOfRowsInSection section: Int) -> Int {
    return items.count
}
```

In the `tableView(_:cellForRowAt:)` method, you will use the array to populate the content of each cell. Each cell will display a different item from the `items` array.

swift

```
func     tableView(_      tableView:    UITableView,
cellForRowAt     indexPath:     IndexPath)     ->
UITableViewCell {
    let                 cell              =
tableView.dequeueReusableCell(withIdentifier:
"cellIdentifier", for: indexPath)
    cell.textLabel?.text = items[indexPath.row]
    return cell
}
```

Example: Displaying a List of Items in a Table View

Let's create a simple app that displays a list of items (such as to-do tasks) in a table view.

Step 1: Setting Up the UI in Storyboard

1. Drag a **UITableView** into your view controller's scene in the storyboard.
2. Create a cell in the table view and give it a **reuse identifier** (e.g., `cellIdentifier`).
3. Add a **UIButton** above the table view that will allow the user to add items to the list.

Step 2: Connecting UI Elements to Code

In **ViewController.swift**, create an array to hold the items and connect the table view to your code:

174

```
swift

import UIKit

class     ViewController:      UIViewController,
UITableViewDataSource, UITableViewDelegate {

    @IBOutlet weak var tableView: UITableView!
    var items = ["Buy groceries", "Walk the dog",
"Read a book"]

    override func viewDidLoad() {
        super.viewDidLoad()
        tableView.dataSource = self
        tableView.delegate = self
    }

    // UITableViewDataSource methods
    func  tableView(_  tableView:  UITableView,
numberOfRowsInSection section: Int) -> Int {
        return items.count
    }

    func  tableView(_  tableView:  UITableView,
cellForRowAt    indexPath:     IndexPath)    ->
UITableViewCell {
        let            cell            =
tableView.dequeueReusableCell(withIdentifier:
"cellIdentifier", for: indexPath)
```

```
        cell.textLabel?.text                =
items[indexPath.row]
        return cell
    }


    // Action for adding a new item
    @IBAction func addItem(_ sender: UIButton) {
        let newItem = "New Task \(items.count +
1)"
        items.append(newItem)
        tableView.reloadData()
    }
}
```

Step 3: Adding New Items to the Table

The addItem method appends a new item to the items array and
then reloads the table view to display the updated list.

1. **UIButton Action**: When the user taps the button, a new
   task is added to the array, and the table view is reloaded
   to show the new item.

2. **Table   View   Data   Source**:   The
   numberOfRowsInSection method returns the number
   of tasks in the array, while cellForRowAt populates
   each cell with the corresponding task.

176

Step 4: Running the App

Now, when you run the app, you'll see a list of tasks displayed in the table view. Each time you tap the "Add Item" button, a new task will be added to the list, and the table view will update to show the new task.

Additional Table View Features

1. **Table View Editing**: You can allow users to delete or reorder items in the table view. To enable this, implement the following methods:

swift

```
// Allow rows to be deleted
func   tableView(_   tableView:   UITableView,
canEditRowAt indexPath: IndexPath) -> Bool {
    return true
}


// Handle deletion of items
func tableView(_ tableView: UITableView, commit
editingStyle:       UITableViewCell.EditingStyle,
forRowAt indexPath: IndexPath) {
    if editingStyle == .delete {
        items.remove(at: indexPath.row)
```

177

```
        tableView.deleteRows(at:      [indexPath],
with: .fade)
    }
}
```

2. **Table View Selection**: You can respond to row selections by implementing the `didSelectRowAt` method. For example, navigating to a detail screen when a task is tapped:

```swift
func    tableView(_    tableView:    UITableView,
didSelectRowAt indexPath: IndexPath) {
    let selectedItem = items[indexPath.row]
    print("Selected item: \(selectedItem)")
}
```

Summary

In this chapter, we covered:

- **UITableView**: A powerful UI component used to display lists of data.
- **UITableViewDataSource**: A protocol that provides data to the table view.
- **UITableViewDelegate**: A protocol that allows you to respond to user actions, such as selecting or deleting rows.

- **Handling Table View Data**: We used an array to store the items and populated the table view using UITableViewDataSource methods.

- **Example**: We built a simple to-do app where users can add tasks to a list and view them in a table view.

Table views are fundamental to creating apps with dynamic content, and understanding how to work with them is essential for iOS development. In the next chapter, we will explore how to handle **search functionality** in iOS, allowing users to filter large sets of data.

CHAPTER 17

WORKING WITH COLLECTION VIEWS

In this chapter, we'll explore **collection views**, which are powerful tools for displaying a grid or a list of items in iOS apps. Collection views are more flexible than table views and allow you to create complex, dynamic layouts, such as photo galleries, shopping grids, and interactive interfaces. We'll cover the basics of collection views, how to customize their layouts, and build a simple **photo gallery app** as a practical example.

Introduction to Collection Views and Their Benefits

A **collection view** is a UI element used to display an ordered or unordered grid of data, with multiple sections and items. It's more flexible and customizable than a table view, making it ideal for displaying content like images, videos, or interactive elements in a variety of layouts.

180

Why Use Collection Views?

- **Dynamic Layouts**: Unlike table views, collection views can have multiple layouts, including grids, custom layouts, and layouts with varying item sizes.
- **Flexible Data Representation**: You can use collection views to represent data in both vertical and horizontal orientations, making them versatile for apps that require dynamic content presentation.
- **Item Customization**: Each item in a collection view can be customized to show images, labels, buttons, or any other custom views.

Basic Components of a Collection View:

- **UICollectionView**: The main container that manages the collection view.
- **UICollectionViewCell**: A reusable container for displaying each item in the collection view.
- **UICollectionViewLayout**: Defines how items are arranged within the collection view (e.g., grid, flow layout).

181

Customizing Collection View Layouts

By default, collection views use the **UICollectionViewFlowLayout**, which arranges items in a single, scrollable line (either vertically or horizontally). However, you can customize this layout to create more complex designs.

UICollectionViewFlowLayout:

- **UICollectionViewFlowLayout** is used to create a grid-like structure with rows and columns.
- You can configure the number of columns, item size, spacing between items, and more.

Configuring Item Size:

You can customize the item size in a flow layout. For example, you can set fixed sizes for items or make them dynamic based on the screen size.

```swift
swift

let layout = UICollectionViewFlowLayout()
layout.itemSize = CGSize(width: 100, height: 100)
// Fixed item size
layout.minimumInteritemSpacing = 10 // Spacing
between items
layout.minimumLineSpacing = 20 // Spacing between
rows
```

182

Custom Layouts:

If you need even more control over how items are arranged, you can create a custom layout by subclassing **UICollectionViewLayout**. This allows you to create complex, non-linear designs, like circular or spiral layouts.

Practical Example: Building a Photo Gallery App

In this example, we'll create a simple **photo gallery app** using a **UICollectionView** to display a grid of images. The app will allow users to tap on an image to view it in full-screen mode.

Step 1: Setting Up the UICollectionView in Storyboard

1. **Drag a UICollectionView** from the Object Library into your view controller's scene in the storyboard.
2. Add a **UICollectionViewCell** inside the collection view and set the **reuse identifier** (e.g., `photoCell`).
3. Set constraints to make the collection view responsive across different screen sizes.
4. Drag a **UIButton** or **UILabel** for a title or to perform additional actions.

Step 2: Configuring the ViewController

In **ViewController.swift**, create an array of photo URLs (or images) to display in the collection view:

swift

```
import UIKit

class     ViewController:     UIViewController,
UICollectionViewDataSource,
UICollectionViewDelegate {

    @IBOutlet    weak    var    collectionView:
UICollectionView!

    let photos = [
        UIImage(named: "photo1"),
        UIImage(named: "photo2"),
        UIImage(named: "photo3"),
        UIImage(named: "photo4"),
        UIImage(named: "photo5")
    ]

    override func viewDidLoad() {
        super.viewDidLoad()
        collectionView.dataSource = self
        collectionView.delegate = self
```

```swift
    // Optional: Customize collection view
layout
    let              layout           =
UICollectionViewFlowLayout()
    layout.itemSize  =  CGSize(width:  120,
height: 120)
    layout.minimumInteritemSpacing = 10
    layout.minimumLineSpacing = 10
    collectionView.collectionViewLayout   =
layout
  }


  // Data source methods
  func    collectionView(_    collectionView:
UICollectionView,          numberOfItemsInSection
section: Int) -> Int {
    return photos.count
  }


  func   collectionView(_    collectionView:
UICollectionView,   cellForItemAt   indexPath:
IndexPath) -> UICollectionViewCell {
    let             cell            =
collectionView.dequeueReusableCell(withIdentifi
er: "photoCell", for: indexPath) as! PhotoCell
    cell.imageView.image            =
photos[indexPath.row]
    return cell
  }
```

185

```
// Delegate method for handling item
selection
func collectionView(_ collectionView:
UICollectionView, didSelectItemAt indexPath:
IndexPath) {
    // Handle the item selection, e.g., show
the image in full screen
    let selectedImage =
photos[indexPath.row]
    showFullScreenImage(selectedImage)
}


// Example function to handle full-screen
image display
func showFullScreenImage(_ image: UIImage?)
{
    let fullScreenImageVC =
FullScreenImageViewController()
    fullScreenImageVC.image = image

navigationController?.pushViewController(fullSc
reenImageVC, animated: true)
    }
}
```

Step 3: Creating a Custom UICollectionViewCell

To customize the collection view cells, create a new UICollectionViewCell subclass (e.g., PhotoCell.swift):

```swift
import UIKit

class PhotoCell: UICollectionViewCell {
    @IBOutlet weak var imageView: UIImageView!

    override func awakeFromNib() {
        super.awakeFromNib()
        // Custom setup for cell
        imageView.layer.cornerRadius = 8
        imageView.layer.masksToBounds = true
    }
}
```

- **PhotoCell** contains an `UIImageView` to display the photo. The cell is customized to have rounded corners.

Step 4: Displaying the Full-Screen Image

Create a new **FullScreenImageViewController** to display the selected image in full-screen mode:

```swift
import UIKit

class           FullScreenImageViewController:
UIViewController {
```

187

```
var image: UIImage?

@IBOutlet weak var imageView: UIImageView!

override func viewDidLoad() {
    super.viewDidLoad()
    imageView.image = image
    imageView.contentMode = .scaleAspectFit
}
}
```

- When a user taps an image in the collection view, the app navigates to this full-screen view where the image is displayed.

Summary of Collection Views

In this chapter, we covered the following key concepts related to **collection views**:

- **UICollectionView**: A flexible, customizable UI element for displaying grid-like or list-like data.
- **UICollectionViewCell**: Represents individual items in the collection view.
- **UICollectionViewFlowLayout**: Used to create simple grid-based layouts with rows and columns.

- **Custom Layouts**: You can subclass **UICollectionViewLayout** to create complex, non-linear layouts.
- **Handling Data**: Using arrays to provide data to the collection view.
- **Example**: We built a photo gallery app where users can view images in a grid and tap to view them in full-screen mode.

Collection views are essential for displaying complex, dynamic data in an organized way. In the next chapter, we'll explore **working with table views and collection views together**, enhancing the functionality of your app.

Are you ready to continue to the next chapter, or would you like to dive deeper into any of the concepts discussed here?

CHAPTER 18

HANDLING DATA WITH CORE DATA

In this chapter, we'll explore **Core Data**, Apple's framework for managing the model layer of your application. Core Data allows you to store, manage, and retrieve data in a structured way. It is especially useful for creating persistent data-driven apps that need to store and retrieve large amounts of data, such as contact lists, to-do lists, and other forms of data that need to persist across app launches. We'll cover the basics of Core Data, how to set it up in your app, and provide a practical example by building a **persistent to-do list app**.

What is Core Data and Why is It Important?

Core Data is a powerful framework that helps you manage the app's data model. It provides a set of tools for handling:

- **Persistent storage**: Saving data on disk so that it can be loaded later.
- **Data models**: Defining the structure of your data (e.g., tasks, users, items).

- **Data querying**: Efficiently fetching data from the persistent store.
- **Data relationships**: Defining relationships between different types of data, such as one-to-many or many-to-many.

Why Use Core Data?

- **Persistence**: Core Data allows you to store data permanently, even after the app is closed and reopened.
- **Performance**: Core Data handles large datasets efficiently with in-memory caching and lazy loading.
- **Complex Data Models**: You can create complex relationships between data objects, such as tasks, users, and categories.
- **Integration with UI**: Core Data integrates well with iOS components like **UITableView** and **UICollectionView** to display data.

Setting Up Core Data in Your App

Setting up Core Data in an iOS app is relatively straightforward. When you create a new project in Xcode, you can enable Core Data during the project setup, or you can manually add Core Data support to an existing project.

Step 1: Enabling Core Data

To enable Core Data in your Xcode project:

1. When creating a new project, check the **Use Core Data** option in the project settings.
2. If you're adding Core Data to an existing project:
   o Add a new **Data Model** file (with the `.xcdatamodeld` extension).
   o Add the **NSPersistentContainer** to the app's delegate.

Here's what the code looks like when setting up the persistent container:

```swift
import CoreData

class AppDelegate: UIResponder, UIApplicationDelegate {

    lazy var persistentContainer: NSPersistentContainer = {
        let container = NSPersistentContainer(name: "ToDoApp") // Name of the Data Model file
```

```
container.loadPersistentStores(completionHandle
r: { (storeDescription, error) in
            if let error = error as NSError? {
                fatalError("Unresolved     error
\(error), \(error.userInfo)")
            }
        })
        return container
    }()


    func saveContext() {
        let              context              =
persistentContainer.viewContext
        if context.hasChanges {
            do {
                try context.save()
            } catch {
                let nserror = error as NSError
                fatalError("Unresolved     error
\(nserror), \(nserror.userInfo)")
            }
        }
    }
}
```

In this code:

- `NSPersistentContainer` is responsible for managing the Core Data stack (i.e., the model, store, and context).
- The `loadPersistentStores` method loads the data from the persistent store into the app's context.

Step 2: Define the Data Model

The data model defines the structure of your data, including entities, attributes, and relationships.

1. Open the **.xcdatamodeld** file in Xcode.
2. Add a new **Entity** (e.g., `Task`).
3. Define **attributes** for the entity, such as `title` (String), `isCompleted` (Boolean), and `dueDate` (Date).
4. Set the **primary key** (e.g., `id` attribute).

Storing and Fetching Data with Core Data

Once you've set up Core Data, you can store and retrieve data using the **NSManagedObjectContext**, which represents the working space for your objects. You'll interact with the context to add, update, delete, and fetch data.

Saving Data:

To add a new task to the persistent store:

194

```swift
func saveTask(title: String, isCompleted: Bool)
{
    let context = (UIApplication.shared.delegate
as! AppDelegate).persistentContainer.viewContext
    let task = Task(context: context)  // Task is
the entity in the data model
    task.title = title
    task.isCompleted = isCompleted
    task.dueDate = Date()

    do {
        try context.save()  // Save changes to
the context
    } catch {
        print("Failed to save task: \(error)")
    }
}
```

In this method:

- We create a new instance of `Task` (which is an `NSManagedObject` subclass).
- We set the properties (`title`, `isCompleted`, and `dueDate`) and save the context to persist the data.

195

Fetching Data:

To fetch data from the persistent store:

swift

```
func fetchTasks() -> [Task] {
    let context = (UIApplication.shared.delegate
as! AppDelegate).persistentContainer.viewContext
    let fetchRequest: NSFetchRequest<Task> =
Task.fetchRequest()  // Fetch all tasks

    do {
        let        tasks       =        try
context.fetch(fetchRequest)  // Fetch tasks from
the context
        return tasks
    } catch {
        print("Failed to fetch tasks: \(error)")
        return []
    }
}
```

In this method:

- We create a **fetch request** for the Task entity.
- We execute the fetch request and return the results as an array of Task objects.

Deleting Data:

To delete a task:

swift

```
func deleteTask(task: Task) {
    let context = (UIApplication.shared.delegate
as! AppDelegate).persistentContainer.viewContext
    context.delete(task)    // Delete the task
object

    do {
        try context.save()    // Save changes to
the context
    } catch {
        print("Failed to delete task: \(error)")
    }
}
```

In this method:

- We call delete() on the context to remove the Task object.
- We save the context to apply the changes to the persistent store.

Example: Creating a Persistent To-Do List App

Now, let's combine everything we've learned to create a simple **to-do list app** that stores tasks using Core Data.

Step 1: Set Up the UI in Storyboard

1. Create a **UITableView** to display the list of tasks.
2. Add a **UIButton** to allow users to add new tasks.
3. Create **UITextField** for entering the task title.
4. Create an **IBOutlet** for the table view and an **IBAction** for the button.

Step 2: Implementing the ViewController

In `ViewController.swift`, use the following code to manage the tasks and interact with Core Data.

```swift
import UIKit
import CoreData

class ViewController: UIViewController, UITableViewDataSource {

    @IBOutlet weak var tableView: UITableView!
    var tasks: [Task] = []
```

```swift
override func viewDidLoad() {
    super.viewDidLoad()
    fetchTasks()
}

// UITableViewDataSource methods
func tableView(_ tableView: UITableView,
numberOfRowsInSection section: Int) -> Int {
    return tasks.count
}

func tableView(_ tableView: UITableView,
cellForRowAt indexPath: IndexPath) ->
UITableViewCell {
    let cell =
tableView.dequeueReusableCell(withIdentifier:
"cellIdentifier", for: indexPath)
    let task = tasks[indexPath.row]
    cell.textLabel?.text = task.title
    return cell
}

// Fetch tasks from Core Data
func fetchTasks() {
    let context =
(UIApplication.shared.delegate as!
AppDelegate).persistentContainer.viewContext
    let fetchRequest: NSFetchRequest<Task> =
Task.fetchRequest()
```

```
        do {
            tasks           =           try
context.fetch(fetchRequest)
            tableView.reloadData()    // Reload
table view with fetched tasks
        } catch {
            print("Failed    to    fetch    tasks:
\(error)")
        }
    }


    // Add a new task
    @IBAction func addTask(_ sender: UIButton) {
        saveTask(title: "New Task", isCompleted:
false)
        fetchTasks()
    }


    // Save a task to Core Data
    func  saveTask(title:  String,  isCompleted:
Bool) {
        let            context            =
(UIApplication.shared.delegate            as!
AppDelegate).persistentContainer.viewContext
        let task = Task(context: context)
        task.title = title
        task.isCompleted = isCompleted
        task.dueDate = Date()
```

```
do {
    try context.save()
} catch {
    print("Failed    to    save    task:
\(error)")
    }
  }
}
```

Step 3: Running the App

When you run the app:

1. The table view will display the list of tasks stored in Core Data.

2. Tapping the "Add Task" button will create a new task and refresh the list.

Summary

In this chapter, we covered:

- **Core Data**: A framework for managing persistent data, providing powerful features for saving, fetching, and deleting data.

- **Setting Up Core Data**: Enabling Core Data in your app and configuring the `NSPersistentContainer`.
- **Storing and Fetching Data**: Using the `NSManagedObjectContext` to store and retrieve data.
- **Example**: Building a persistent to-do list app that saves tasks in Core Data and displays them in a `UITableView`.

Core Data is an essential tool for managing app data that persists across app launches. In the next chapter, we will explore **working with advanced UI elements** like custom table view cells, collection view cells, and more.

Are you ready to move on to the next chapter, or would you like more details on any of the concepts discussed here?

CHAPTER 19

NETWORKING AND APIS IN SWIFT

In this chapter, we'll explore how to handle networking in iOS and make requests to external **APIs** (Application Programming Interfaces) to retrieve data over the internet. This is a key aspect of many apps that need to interact with web services, such as pulling data from a weather service, retrieving images, or submitting user information to a server. We will focus on using **URLSession** to make network requests and process **JSON** data. As a practical example, we'll build a **weather app** that fetches weather data from an API and displays it in the app.

Introduction to Networking in iOS

Networking in iOS allows your app to communicate with remote servers, fetch data, and send data back. Whether it's pulling information from a web service, downloading files, or uploading user data, networking is essential for many apps.

What Is an API?

An **API** is a set of rules that allows one software application to interact with another. In mobile development, an API typically allows an app to fetch data or interact with a server. APIs often return data in **JSON** (JavaScript Object Notation) format, which is a lightweight data format that is easy to parse and work with in Swift.

What Is URLSession?

`URLSession` is the primary class used in iOS to make network requests. It provides a variety of methods for sending and receiving data from the web, including:

- **GET requests**: Fetching data from a server.
- **POST requests**: Sending data to a server.
- **Download and Upload tasks**: For downloading and uploading files.

Using URLSession to Make Network Requests

The `URLSession` class allows you to make network requests in a few simple steps:

1. **Create a URL**: The destination for your request.

2. **Create a URLRequest**: (Optional) Customize the request (e.g., method, headers).

3. **Create a data task**: A task that fetches data asynchronously.

4. **Handle the response**: Process the server's response or error.

Step-by-Step Example of a GET Request Using URLSession

Let's create a simple network request to fetch data from an API:

```swift
import UIKit

class ViewController: UIViewController {

    override func viewDidLoad() {
        super.viewDidLoad()
        fetchWeatherData()
    }

    func fetchWeatherData() {
        let            urlString            =
"https://api.openweathermap.org/data/2.5/weathe
r?q=London&appid=YOUR_API_KEY"
        guard let url = URL(string: urlString)
else {
            print("Invalid URL")
```

205

```
        return
    }


    // Create a URLSession data task to fetch
data from the API
    let              task              =
URLSession.shared.dataTask(with:  url)  {  data,
response, error in
        // Handle errors
        if let error = error {
            print("Error    fetching    data:
\(error)")
            return
        }


        // Check the response status
        guard let httpResponse = response as?
HTTPURLResponse, httpResponse.statusCode == 200
else {
            print("Server error")
            return
        }


        // Process the received data
        if let data = data {
            self.parseWeatherData(data)
        }
    }
```

```
    task.resume()     // Start the network
request
    }


    // Parse the JSON data received from the API
    func parseWeatherData(_ data: Data) {
        do {
            // Decode the JSON response into a
Swift object
            let decoder = JSONDecoder()
            let      weather      =        try
decoder.decode(WeatherResponse.self, from: data)
            print("Weather  in  \(weather.name):
\(weather.main.temp)°C")
        } catch {
            print("Error      parsing      JSON:
\(error)")
        }
    }
}
```

Explanation:

- **URLSession**: We create a shared session using `URLSession.shared` and use `dataTask(with:)` to initiate the request.
- **Completion Handler**: The completion handler receives the data, response, and error. If an error occurs, we print the error message.

207

- **Status Code**: We check if the server response status code is 200 (OK) before processing the data.
- **JSON Parsing**: We use **JSONDecoder** to decode the received JSON data into a Swift struct.

WeatherResponse Struct:

To parse the JSON, we define a struct that conforms to Decodable:

swift

```swift
struct WeatherResponse: Decodable {
    let name: String  // City name
    let main: MainWeather  // Weather data

    struct MainWeather: Decodable {
        let temp: Double  // Temperature in
Celsius
    }
}
```

This struct matches the structure of the JSON response from the weather API.

Working with JSON Data and APIs

When dealing with APIs, the data you receive is typically in **JSON** format. JSON is an easy-to-use, human-readable data format. You can easily parse JSON data in Swift using **Codable** (a protocol that combines `Encodable` and `Decodable`).

JSON Example:

Here's an example of a JSON response from a weather API:

json

```
{
    "name": "London",
    "main": {
        "temp": 293.15
    }
}
```

We can map this JSON structure to a Swift struct by defining properties that match the keys in the JSON.

Handling Errors in Networking Requests:

It's essential to handle potential errors in networking requests, such as:

- **Network connectivity issues**.

- **Invalid URLs**.
- **Server errors** (e.g., a status code other than 200).
- **Data parsing errors**.

In the previous code, we handled errors by checking for:

- Errors in the `dataTask` completion handler.
- The HTTP status code of the response.
- Parsing errors when decoding the JSON.

Example: Building a Weather App that Pulls Data from an API

Let's expand the previous example and build a **simple weather app** that shows the current temperature of a city. The app will use **OpenWeatherMap API** to fetch the weather data and display it.

Step 1: Create the User Interface

In **Main.storyboard**:

1. Add a **UITextField** for entering the city name.
2. Add a **UIButton** to trigger the weather request.
3. Add a **UILabel** to display the temperature.

Step 2: Implementing the ViewController

In **ViewController.swift**, set up the UI and network request:

```swift

import UIKit

class ViewController: UIViewController {

    @IBOutlet weak var cityTextField: UITextField!
    @IBOutlet weak var temperatureLabel: UILabel!

    override func viewDidLoad() {
        super.viewDidLoad()
    }

    @IBAction func getWeatherTapped(_ sender: UIButton) {
        guard let city = cityTextField.text, !city.isEmpty else {
            print("Please enter a city name")
            return
        }

        fetchWeatherData(for: city)
    }

    func fetchWeatherData(for city: String) {
        let apiKey = "YOUR_API_KEY"
```

```swift
        let               urlString          =
"https://api.openweathermap.org/data/2.5/weathe
r?q=\(city)&appid=\(apiKey)&units=metric"
        guard let url = URL(string: urlString)
else {
            print("Invalid URL")
            return
        }

        // Create a URLSession data task
        let               task               =
URLSession.shared.dataTask(with: url) { data,
response, error in
            if let error = error {
                print("Error    fetching   data:
\(error)")
                return
            }

            guard let data = data else {
                print("No data received")
                return
            }

            // Parse the JSON data
            self.parseWeatherData(data)
        }
```

```
        task.resume()    // Start the network
request
    }


    func parseWeatherData(_ data: Data) {
        do {
            let decoder = JSONDecoder()
            let weatherResponse    =    try
decoder.decode(WeatherResponse.self, from: data)


            DispatchQueue.main.async {
                self.temperatureLabel.text    =
"Temperature: \(weatherResponse.main.temp)°C"
            }
        } catch {
            print("Error    parsing    JSON:
\(error)")
        }
    }
}
```

Explanation:

- The **UITextField** allows the user to enter a city name.
- The **UIButton** triggers the API request to fetch weather data.
- The **UILabel** displays the temperature once the data is fetched.

Step 3: Handle Errors and Display Results

We've added basic error handling, such as checking for an empty city name and handling potential networking errors. Once the weather data is fetched and parsed, we update the label with the temperature.

Summary

In this chapter, we learned:

- **Networking in iOS**: How to use `URLSession` to make network requests and retrieve data from APIs.
- **JSON Parsing**: Using `JSONDecoder` to decode JSON data into Swift structs that conform to `Decodable`.
- **Building a Weather App**: A practical example where we used a weather API to display the current temperature for a city.

Networking and APIs are essential for building apps that interact with the internet, and understanding how to fetch and parse data will be key in creating data-driven apps. In the next chapter, we'll explore **handling background tasks and notifications** in iOS to keep your app responsive and up-to-date even when it's not in the foreground.

CHAPTER 20

INTRODUCTION TO SWIFTUI

In this chapter, we will introduce **SwiftUI**, Apple's declarative framework for building user interfaces across all Apple platforms. SwiftUI allows you to create UI elements and manage data binding in a more streamlined and intuitive way than UIKit. We'll explore how SwiftUI differs from UIKit, build a basic SwiftUI interface, and learn how to bind data to SwiftUI views. Finally, we'll walk through an example of creating a simple app using SwiftUI.

Introduction to SwiftUI and How It Differs from UIKit

UIKit has been the standard framework for building iOS user interfaces for many years. It uses an **imperative** programming style, where developers must specify the detailed steps to create and update UI elements. While UIKit is powerful, it can sometimes be verbose and challenging to maintain as the complexity of an app increases.

SwiftUI, on the other hand, is **declarative**, meaning you describe what the user interface should do, and SwiftUI automatically handles the updates. SwiftUI is designed to simplify the process of building UI, and it integrates seamlessly with data binding and state management, making it easier to develop dynamic, responsive apps.

Key Differences Between SwiftUI and UIKit:

- **Declarative vs. Imperative**: In SwiftUI, you describe your UI in terms of the data it displays, and SwiftUI updates the UI when the data changes. In UIKit, you explicitly manipulate UI elements.
- **Data Binding**: SwiftUI allows you to easily bind data to views, ensuring that the UI is automatically updated when the data changes. UIKit requires manual updates to the UI when data changes.
- **Code Readability**: SwiftUI typically results in cleaner, more readable code, as it reduces the need for repetitive UI updates.
- **Cross-Platform**: SwiftUI is designed to work across all Apple platforms (iOS, macOS, watchOS, tvOS), making it easier to build apps for multiple platforms using a single codebase.

Building a Basic SwiftUI Interface

SwiftUI uses **views** to define UI elements, and views are created using a combination of built-in view types (e.g., `Text`, `Button`, `VStack`, `HStack`, `List`) and modifiers to style and arrange them.

Example: A Simple Text Label in SwiftUI
swift

```swift
import SwiftUI

struct ContentView: View {
    var body: some View {
        Text("Hello, SwiftUI!")
            .font(.largeTitle)
            .padding()
    }
}
```

In this example:

- `ContentView` is a SwiftUI view that conforms to the `View` protocol.
- The `body` property contains a `Text` view with a modifier `.font(.largeTitle)` to set the font size and `.padding()` to add padding around the text.

Key Concepts in SwiftUI:

- **View**: A protocol that defines how the user interface is presented. Every SwiftUI component (button, label, image, etc.) is a view.
- **Modifiers**: Functions that modify the appearance or behavior of views (e.g., `.padding()`, `.font()`, `.background()`).
- **VStack, HStack, ZStack**: Containers used to arrange views vertically, horizontally, or stacked on top of each other.
- **State**: A property that stores data for a view, and when this data changes, SwiftUI automatically updates the view.

Binding Data in SwiftUI Views

One of the most powerful features of SwiftUI is its data binding system. **Binding** allows you to create a connection between your data and your views. When the data changes, the view automatically updates to reflect the new data.

Using @State for Local State Management

The @State property wrapper is used to declare local state variables in SwiftUI. It allows you to bind data to a view and automatically update the view when the data changes.

```swift
import SwiftUI

struct ContentView: View {
    @State private var count = 0

    var body: some View {
        VStack {
            Text("Count: \(count)")
                .font(.title)
                .padding()

            Button(action: {
                count += 1
            }) {
                Text("Increment")
                    .padding()
                    .background(Color.blue)
                    .foregroundColor(.white)
                    .cornerRadius(10)
            }
        }
```

```
        }
    }
```

In this example:

- The `@State` property wrapper creates a local state variable `count`.
- The `Text` view displays the value of `count`.
- The `Button` updates the value of `count` when tapped, and SwiftUI automatically updates the displayed count.

Using `@Binding` for External State

Sometimes, you need to pass data between views. You can use the `@Binding` property wrapper to bind a value from a parent view to a child view.

```swift
import SwiftUI

struct ParentView: View {
    @State private var count = 0

    var body: some View {
        ChildView(count: $count)   // Passing a binding to the child view
    }
}
```

```
struct ChildView: View {
    @Binding var count: Int   // Binding to the
parent's state

    var body: some View {
        Button(action: {
            count += 1
        }) {
            Text("Increment")
        }
    }
}
```

In this example:

- The `ParentView` has a state variable `count`, and it passes a **binding** to `ChildView` using `$count`.
- The `ChildView` uses the `@Binding` property wrapper to update the parent's `count` directly.

Example: Creating a Simple SwiftUI-Based App

Now, let's create a simple **SwiftUI-based app** that allows the user to input their name and display a personalized greeting. This example will showcase how to use text fields, buttons, and data binding in SwiftUI.

Step 1: Set Up the User Interface

We will create a `TextField` for the user to enter their name, a `Button` to submit the name, and a `Text` view to display a personalized greeting.

```swift
import SwiftUI

struct ContentView: View {
    @State private var name = ""
    @State private var greeting = ""

    var body: some View {
        VStack {
            TextField("Enter your name", text: $name)
                .padding()

.textFieldStyle(RoundedBorderTextFieldStyle())

            Button(action: {
                greeting = "Hello, \(name)!"
            }) {
                Text("Greet Me")
                    .padding()
                    .background(Color.blue)
                    .foregroundColor(.white)
```

```
                    .cornerRadius(10)
            }
            .padding()

            Text(greeting)
                .font(.title)
                .padding()
        }
        .padding()
    }
}
```

Step 2: Explanation of the Code

- **@State**: We use @State to declare the name and greeting variables, which store the input and the generated greeting.
- **TextField**: Allows the user to enter their name. The value is bound to the name variable using $name.
- **Button**: When the button is tapped, it updates the greeting variable with a personalized message.
- **Text**: Displays the greeting.

Step 3: Running the App

When the app is run:

- The user enters their name in the text field.

- When the "Greet Me" button is tapped, the app displays a greeting message below the button.

Summary

In this chapter, we learned about **SwiftUI**, Apple's declarative framework for building user interfaces:

- **SwiftUI** uses a declarative approach, meaning you describe what the UI should look like, and SwiftUI automatically handles the layout and updates.
- **Views** are the building blocks of SwiftUI apps, and we use views like `Text`, `Button`, and `TextField` to create the UI.
- **Data Binding** allows you to connect your data to the UI, ensuring that when the data changes, the UI updates automatically.
- We built a **simple SwiftUI-based app** to demonstrate how to use text fields, buttons, and data binding in SwiftUI.

SwiftUI is a powerful and efficient framework for building modern iOS apps with less code. In the next chapter, we will explore **advanced SwiftUI concepts** like lists, navigation, and custom components to create more complex apps.

CHAPTER 21

ANIMATIONS AND TRANSITIONS IN IOS

In this chapter, we'll explore how to use **animations** and **transitions** in iOS to enhance the user experience. Animations are a great way to make your app feel dynamic and interactive, providing visual feedback for user actions or drawing attention to specific elements on the screen. We will cover the basics of animations in iOS, including how to use **UIView animations** and **Core Animation**. Additionally, we'll learn how to create **custom transitions** between screens. We'll also walk through an example of animating a loading spinner in an app.

Introduction to Animations in iOS

Animations are used to modify the properties of a view over time, creating smooth transitions and effects. Whether you are animating a simple button tap or creating complex transitions between views, iOS provides powerful tools to create animations that bring your app's interface to life.

Types of Animations in iOS:

1. **UIView Animations**: Simple, block-based animations that allow you to animate properties such as frame, bounds, alpha, and transform.

2. **Core Animation**: A lower-level framework that allows for more complex animations, including 2D and 3D transformations, and advanced timing functions.

3. **Custom Transitions**: Animations that control how views transition between each other, such as pushing a view or presenting a modal.

Why Use Animations?

- **Enhance User Experience**: Animations can make an app feel more responsive and interactive.

- **Draw Attention**: Use animations to direct the user's focus to a particular UI element.

- **Provide Feedback**: Animations can show progress, completion, or indicate changes, such as a loading spinner.

226

Using UIView Animations and Core Animation

UIView Animations

`UIView` provides simple animations that are easy to use and ideal for animating properties like frame, alpha, rotation, and opacity. The syntax for `UIView` animations is clean and simple, using a block-based approach.

Basic UIView Animation:

Here's an example of animating a view's position using `UIView.animate`:

```swift
swift

import UIKit

class ViewController: UIViewController {

    @IBOutlet weak var boxView: UIView!

    override func viewDidLoad() {
        super.viewDidLoad()

        // Example of animating a view
        animateView()
    }

    func animateView() {
```

227

```
        // Animate position change of boxView
        UIView.animate(withDuration:          1.0,
animations: {
            self.boxView.frame.origin.x += 200
            self.boxView.alpha = 0.5  // Fade out
as it moves
        }) { (finished) in
            print("Animation Complete!")
        }
    }
}
```

Explanation:

- The `UIView.animate` function is used to animate changes in the properties of `boxView`.
- We animate its horizontal position (`frame.origin.x`) and set its alpha value (opacity).
- The animation lasts 1 second, and once the animation is complete, the completion handler prints "Animation Complete!"

Animating Multiple Properties:

You can animate multiple properties simultaneously:

swift

```
UIView.animate(withDuration: 1.0, animations: {
```

```
    self.boxView.transform                =
CGAffineTransform(rotationAngle:  .pi  /  4)  //
Rotate the view
    self.boxView.frame.origin.y  += 100 // Move
the view vertically
})
```

In this example:

- We rotate the view by 45 degrees (`.pi / 4`).
- We also move it vertically by 100 points.

Core Animation

Core Animation provides more flexibility and power for animations, especially for complex transitions, 3D animations, and advanced timing.

Basic Core Animation Example:

Let's use Core Animation to animate a layer's position:

```swift
import UIKit

class ViewController: UIViewController {

    @IBOutlet weak var boxView: UIView!
```

```
    override func viewDidLoad() {
        super.viewDidLoad()

        // Add a shadow to the box
        boxView.layer.shadowColor              =
UIColor.black.cgColor
        boxView.layer.shadowOpacity = 0.5
        boxView.layer.shadowOffset             =
CGSize(width: 5, height: 5)
        boxView.layer.shadowRadius = 10

        // Animate the box with Core Animation
        animateLayer()
    }

    func animateLayer() {
        // Create the animation
        let              animation              =
CABasicAnimation(keyPath: "position.x")
        animation.fromValue                    =
boxView.layer.position.x
        animation.toValue                      =
boxView.layer.position.x + 200
        animation.duration = 1.0

        // Add the animation to the layer
        boxView.layer.add(animation,     forKey:
"positionAnimation")
```

```
        // Update the actual layer position after
the animation completes
        boxView.layer.position.x += 200
    }
}
```

Explanation:

- `CABasicAnimation` is used for animating a single property, in this case, the `position.x` property of the `boxView`'s layer.
- `fromValue` and `toValue` define the start and end values of the animation.
- The animation is added to the layer, and once the animation is complete, the actual position is updated.

Custom Transitions Between Screens

In iOS, **custom transitions** allow you to control how views appear or disappear when moving between different screens (view controllers). You can define your own animations for pushing, presenting, or dismissing view controllers.

Using UIViewControllerAnimatedTransitioning:

To create a custom transition, you need to implement the `UIViewControllerAnimatedTransitioning` protocol. This allows you to define the animation for a transition.

231

1. Create a custom transition class that conforms to UIViewControllerAnimatedTransitioning.

```swift
import UIKit

class CustomTransition: NSObject, UIViewControllerAnimatedTransitioning {

    func transitionDuration(using transitionContext: UIViewControllerContextTransitioning?) -> TimeInterval {
        return 0.5  // Duration of the transition
    }

    func animateTransition(using transitionContext: UIViewControllerContextTransitioning) {
        let fromView = transitionContext.view(forKey: .from)!
        let toView = transitionContext.view(forKey: .to)!

        let containerView = transitionContext.containerView
        containerView.addSubview(toView)
```

232

```
        // Set the initial state for the
animation (e.g., slide from the right)
        toView.frame          =          CGRect(x:
containerView.frame.width,     y:    0,    width:
containerView.frame.width,               height:
containerView.frame.height)


        // Animate the transition
        UIView.animate(withDuration:
transitionDuration(using:     transitionContext),
animations: {
            fromView.frame    =    CGRect(x:    -
containerView.frame.width,     y:    0,    width:
containerView.frame.width,               height:
containerView.frame.height)
            toView.frame = CGRect(x:  0,  y:  0,
width:     containerView.frame.width,     height:
containerView.frame.height)
        }) { (completed) in

transitionContext.completeTransition(completed)
        }
    }
}
```

Explanation:

- In the `animateTransition` method, we define how the `fromView` and `toView` will move during the transition.

233

- The transition makes the current view slide out to the left while the new view slides in from the right.

2. Implement the transition when presenting or pushing a view controller:

```swift
let customTransition = CustomTransition()
let                transitionDelegate                =
CustomTransitionDelegate()

let viewController = NextViewController()
viewController.transitioningDelegate                =
transitionDelegate
present(viewController,        animated:        true,
completion: nil)
```

In this example:

- We use the custom transition for presenting a new view controller. The transition delegate controls the animation that happens during the presentation.

Example: Animating a Loading Spinner in an App

One of the most common animations in apps is a **loading spinner**. A loading spinner is useful when you want to show the user that a process is in progress.

Step 1: Create the Loading Spinner

You can use **UIActivityIndicatorView** to display a loading spinner.

```swift
import UIKit

class ViewController: UIViewController {

    let              activityIndicator              =
UIActivityIndicatorView(style: .large)

    override func viewDidLoad() {
        super.viewDidLoad()

        // Set up the activity indicator
        activityIndicator.center = view.center
        activityIndicator.hidesWhenStopped     =
true
        view.addSubview(activityIndicator)
    }
```

235

```swift
func startLoading() {
    activityIndicator.startAnimating()

    // Simulate a task by delaying the stop
    of the activity indicator
    DispatchQueue.main.asyncAfter(deadline:
    .now() + 3.0) {
        self.stopLoading()
    }
}

func stopLoading() {
    activityIndicator.stopAnimating()
}
}
```

Step 2: Explanation

- We create an `UIActivityIndicatorView` and add it to the view.
- The `startLoading()` method starts the spinner, and `stopLoading()` stops it.
- In this example, we simulate a task by using `DispatchQueue.main.asyncAfter` to stop the spinner after 3 seconds.

Step 3: Running the App

When the app runs, the spinner will appear in the center of the screen and spin for 3 seconds before stopping.

Summary

In this chapter, we covered:

- **Animations in iOS**: How animations can improve the user experience by providing visual feedback and drawing attention to UI elements.
- **UIView Animations**: A simple, block-based way to animate view properties like position, size, and alpha.
- **Core Animation**: A powerful framework for advanced animations, including animating layers and complex transitions.
- **Custom Transitions**: How to create custom animations for navigating between screens.
- **Example**: We built a simple app that shows how to animate a loading spinner and perform basic animations with `UIActivityIndicatorView`.

In the next chapter, we'll dive deeper into **working with gestures**, allowing users to interact with your app using taps, swipes, and pinches.

CHAPTER 22

DEBUGGING AND TESTING IN XCODE

In this chapter, we'll explore the essential tools and techniques for **debugging** and **testing** in Xcode. As your app becomes more complex, you'll need effective ways to troubleshoot issues and ensure that your app works correctly across different scenarios. We'll learn how to use **breakpoints** and **debugging tools** in Xcode, introduce **unit testing** in Swift, and show how to write and run tests to ensure the reliability of your code. Finally, we'll go through an example of writing unit tests for a **simple calculator app**.

Using Breakpoints and Debugging Tools in Xcode

Debugging is an essential part of the development process, allowing you to identify and fix issues in your code. Xcode provides powerful debugging tools, including **breakpoints**, **LLDB commands**, and the **debug area** to help you trace the flow of your app and inspect its state.

Breakpoints in Xcode

A **breakpoint** is a marker in your code where execution pauses, allowing you to inspect the values of variables, step through the code, and analyze the program's flow.

Setting Breakpoints:

1. Click on the gutter (the area to the left of your code) next to the line where you want to set the breakpoint. A blue arrow will appear.
2. When the code execution reaches that line during debugging, the app will pause at the breakpoint.

Common Debugging Tools:

1. **LLDB Console**: Use the LLDB (Low-Level Debugger) console to interact with the app's runtime. You can use commands like `po` (print object) to inspect variables, `p` (print) to evaluate expressions, and `bt` (backtrace) to get a stack trace.

   Example:

   ```sh
   po myVariable  // Prints the value of the
   variable
   ```

```
p myObject.property  // Prints a specific
property of an object
```

2. **Variable Inspection**: When the app pauses at a breakpoint, you can hover over variables to see their values. You can also view all variables in the **variables view**.

3. **Step Through Code**: Use the buttons in the debug area to step through your code:
   - **Step Over**: Move to the next line of code.
   - **Step Into**: Move into the function being called.
   - **Step Out**: Move out of the current function.

4. **Watch Variables**: You can set "watchpoints" to monitor the value of a specific variable while debugging. This will help you identify when the variable's value changes unexpectedly.

Introduction to Unit Testing in Swift

Unit testing ensures that your individual pieces of code (usually functions or methods) work as expected. In Swift, you write unit tests using the **XCTest** framework. Unit tests are important for verifying the behavior of your code and ensuring that future changes don't introduce bugs.

Why Write Unit Tests?

- **Verify Functionality**: Unit tests help ensure that individual components of your app work as expected.
- **Catch Errors Early**: Writing tests early can catch bugs before they make it to production.
- **Facilitate Refactoring**: Unit tests give you confidence that your code is still working correctly after making changes or refactoring.

XCTest Framework:

XCTest provides tools for creating test cases, asserting values, and running tests within the Xcode test suite. It's integrated directly into Xcode, allowing you to write and run tests alongside your code.

1. **Create Test Targets**: Xcode automatically creates a test target when you create a new project. You can add new test classes to your project by creating a new **Test Case Class**.
2. **Test Case Class**: A test case class is a subclass of XCTestCase and contains test methods that start with the test prefix. These methods are automatically executed when you run the tests.

241

Writing and Running Tests for Your App

Step 1: Creating a Test Case Class

To create unit tests, navigate to **File > New > Target**, and select **iOS Unit Testing Bundle**. This will create a test target in your project where you can add your test methods.

Here's an example of a basic test case class:

swift

```swift
import XCTest
@testable import MyApp

class CalculatorTests: XCTestCase {

    var calculator: Calculator!

    override func setUp() {
        super.setUp()
        calculator = Calculator()  // Initialize
the object you want to test
    }

    override func tearDown() {
        calculator = nil  // Clean up after each
test
        super.tearDown()
    }
```

```
func testAddition() {
    let result = calculator.add(3, 5)
    XCTAssertEqual(result, 8, "Expected 3 +
5 to equal 8")
}

func testSubtraction() {
    let result = calculator.subtract(10, 4)
    XCTAssertEqual(result, 6, "Expected 10 -
4 to equal 6")
}
}
```

Explanation:

- **setUp()**: This method is called before each test method is executed. Use it to initialize objects or variables you need for testing.
- **tearDown()**: This method is called after each test method is executed. Use it to clean up any resources.
- **testAddition()**: A test method that checks if the `add` method in the `Calculator` class returns the expected result. `XCTAssertEqual` verifies that the result matches the expected value.
- **testSubtraction()**: A test method that checks the `subtract` method.

1. **Run Tests**: To run all tests, select **Product > Test** (or use the shortcut `Cmd+U`).
2. **Test Results**: Xcode will run the tests and display the results in the **Test Navigator**. Green checkmarks indicate successful tests, while red indicators show failed tests.
3. **Test Output**: If a test fails, Xcode provides a detailed error message, showing the expected value versus the actual result.

Step 3: Adding More Tests

You can write additional test methods for various scenarios:

-   **Edge cases**: Test inputs like empty strings, negative numbers, or large values.
-   **Performance tests**: Use `XCTMeasure` to test the performance of a specific block of code.

Example of performance testing:

```swift
func testPerformanceExample() {
    self.measure {
        let _ = calculator.add(1000, 1000)
    }
```

244

```
}
```

Example: Writing Tests for a Simple Calculator App

Let's write tests for a simple **calculator app** with basic operations like addition, subtraction, multiplication, and division.

Step 1: Calculator Class

Here's a simple `Calculator` class:

swift

```swift
class Calculator {

    func add(_ a: Int, _ b: Int) -> Int {
        return a + b
    }

    func subtract(_ a: Int, _ b: Int) -> Int {
        return a - b
    }

    func multiply(_ a: Int, _ b: Int) -> Int {
        return a * b
    }

    func divide(_ a: Int, _ b: Int) -> Int? {
        guard b != 0 else {
```

245

```
                return nil  // Cannot divide by zero
        }
        return a / b
    }
}
```

Step 2: Writing Unit Tests

Now, let's write tests for the `Calculator` class.

```swift
import XCTest
@testable import MyApp

class CalculatorTests: XCTestCase {

    var calculator: Calculator!

    override func setUp() {
        super.setUp()
        calculator = Calculator()
    }

    override func tearDown() {
        calculator = nil
        super.tearDown()
    }

    func testAddition() {
```

246

```
        XCTAssertEqual(calculator.add(3, 5), 8)
        XCTAssertEqual(calculator.add(-3, 5), 2)
    }


    func testSubtraction() {
        XCTAssertEqual(calculator.subtract(10,
4), 6)
        XCTAssertEqual(calculator.subtract(5,
10), -5)
    }


    func testMultiplication() {
        XCTAssertEqual(calculator.multiply(3,
5), 15)
        XCTAssertEqual(calculator.multiply(0,
5), 0)
    }


    func testDivision() {
        XCTAssertEqual(calculator.divide(10, 2),
5)
        XCTAssertNil(calculator.divide(10,    0))
// Division by zero should return nil
    }
}
```

In these tests:

- **Addition, subtraction, multiplication**: We test normal cases and edge cases like negative numbers or zero.

- **Division**: We check both valid division and division by zero (which should return `nil`).

Summary

In this chapter, we learned about:

- **Debugging in Xcode**: Using breakpoints and the debugger to troubleshoot your app and inspect variables.
- **Unit Testing in Swift**: Introduction to writing unit tests using the `XCTest` framework to verify your code's functionality.
- **Writing and Running Tests**: Creating test methods to verify different parts of your app, and using `XCTAssert` functions to check the expected output.
- **Example**: Writing tests for a simple calculator app, covering addition, subtraction, multiplication, and division.

Testing and debugging are essential parts of ensuring your app works as expected and maintaining its reliability. In the next chapter, we will explore **working with user authentication** in iOS apps, including login and registration workflows.

248

CHAPTER 23

MEMORY MANAGEMENT IN SWIFT

In this chapter, we will explore **memory management** in Swift, which is crucial for building efficient, high-performance apps. Improper memory management can lead to memory leaks, excessive memory usage, and even app crashes. Swift uses **Automatic Reference Counting (ARC)** to manage memory, which is different from manual memory management techniques used in other languages. We'll cover how ARC works, the difference between **strong**, **weak**, and **unowned** references, and how to avoid memory leaks. We'll also look at a real-world example of managing memory in a **photo gallery app**.

Understanding Memory Management in Swift

Memory management in Swift is handled by **Automatic Reference Counting (ARC)**. ARC automatically tracks and manages the memory used by your app by keeping track of the number of references to each object. When there are no more references to an object, ARC frees the memory used by that object.

How ARC Works:

- Every time an object is created, ARC assigns a **reference count** to it. The reference count tracks how many references (or pointers) there are to that object.
- When an object's reference count reaches zero (i.e., no references to the object remain), ARC automatically deallocates the object, freeing the memory it used.

However, while ARC is automatic, it's important to manage references properly, as certain patterns can lead to memory management problems, such as **retain cycles** (strong reference cycles), which prevent objects from being deallocated.

Automatic Reference Counting (ARC) and Strong, Weak, and Unowned References

ARC automatically manages the reference count of objects, but you control whether the reference is **strong**, **weak**, or **unowned**. Understanding these reference types is essential for effective memory management.

Strong References:

- A **strong reference** means that the reference count of the object is incremented when a reference to it is created.

The object will not be deallocated as long as there is at least one strong reference to it.

- **By default**, all references in Swift are **strong**.

Example:

```swift
swift

class MyClass {
    var name: String
    init(name: String) {
        self.name = name
    }
}

var object1 = MyClass(name: "Example") // Strong reference to the object
```

In this example, `object1` holds a strong reference to an instance of `MyClass`. The object will remain in memory as long as `object1` exists.

Weak References:

- A **weak reference** allows an object to be deallocated when no strong references to it remain. Weak references do not retain objects and thus do not increase the reference count.

251

- **Weak references** are typically used in **delegation patterns** or to avoid **retain cycles** in closures.

Key Characteristics:

- Weak references are always optional (`nil` when the object is deallocated).
- Suitable for **delegate** references or when you want to avoid retain cycles in closures.

Example:

```swift
class MyClass {
    var name: String
    init(name: String) {
        self.name = name
    }
}


class AnotherClass {
    weak var myObject: MyClass?    // Weak reference
}
```

In this example, the `myObject` reference is weak, so if there are no strong references to the `MyClass` object, it will be deallocated, and `myObject` will automatically be set to `nil`.

Unowned References:

- An **unowned reference** is similar to a weak reference, but it is **non-optional**. It is used when you know that the referenced object will always exist as long as the object holding the unowned reference exists.
- Unowned references do not increase the reference count, but they do assume that the referenced object will not be deallocated as long as the object holding the reference is alive.

Key Characteristics:

- Unowned references are non-optional.
- Used for references between objects that have a **parent-child** relationship (e.g., a view controller and its subview).

Example:

swift

```
class MyClass {
    var name: String
    init(name: String) {
        self.name = name
    }
}
```

```
class AnotherClass {
    unowned var myObject: MyClass   // Unowned
reference
    init(myObject: MyClass) {
        self.myObject = myObject
    }
}
```

In this case, `myObject` is unowned. The object it references will not be deallocated until the object holding the unowned reference is deallocated.

Avoiding Memory Leaks

A **memory leak** occurs when an object is not deallocated from memory, usually due to a **retain cycle**. Retain cycles happen when two objects hold strong references to each other, preventing either of them from being deallocated.

Retain Cycles in Closures:

Closures in Swift capture variables from their surrounding context. When a closure captures `self` strongly, it can create a retain cycle if `self` also holds a strong reference to the closure. This prevents both the closure and `self` from being deallocated.

Example of Retain Cycle in a Closure:

```swift
swift

class MyClass {
    var name = "Example"

    var closure: (() -> Void)?

    func createClosure() {
        closure = {
            print(self.name)    // Captures self strongly, causing a retain cycle
        }
    }
}
```

In this example, the closure captures `self` strongly, which creates a retain cycle because the class instance also holds a strong reference to the closure.

Breaking the Retain Cycle:

To break a retain cycle in closures, you can use **weak** or **unowned** references when capturing `self`.

Fixing the Retain Cycle with `weak`:

```swift
swift

class MyClass {
```

```
    var name = "Example"

    var closure: (() -> Void)?

    func createClosure() {
        closure = { [weak self] in
            print(self?.name ?? "Unknown")    //
Weak reference to self
        }
    }
}
```

Using [weak self] in the capture list ensures that the closure does not hold a strong reference to self, allowing the object to be deallocated properly.

Example: Managing Memory in a Photo Gallery App

Let's look at an example of managing memory in a **photo gallery app**. In this app, each photo object has a strong reference to its image, and we will manage these references properly to avoid memory leaks.

Step 1: Photo Model
swift

```
class Photo {
    var imageName: String
```

```swift
var image: UIImage?

init(imageName: String) {
    self.imageName = imageName
    self.image = UIImage(named: imageName)
}
}
```

Step 2: View Controller with Strong and Weak References

In the view controller, we want to display a list of photos. We will hold the photo objects in an array, and when the user taps on a photo, we'll use a closure to display it in full-screen. We must ensure that we use **weak** references in closures to avoid retain cycles.

```swift
swift

class                    PhotoGalleryViewController:
UIViewController {

    var photos: [Photo] = []

    override func viewDidLoad() {
        super.viewDidLoad()

        // Create some sample photos
        photos.append(Photo(imageName:
"photo1"))
```

```
        photos.append(Photo(imageName:
"photo2"))
        photos.append(Photo(imageName:
"photo3"))
    }


    func displayPhoto(index: Int) {
        let selectedPhoto = photos[index]

        // Example of weak reference in closure
        showFullScreenPhoto(photo:
selectedPhoto) { [weak self] in
            self?.dismiss(animated:        true,
completion: nil)
        }
    }


    func    showFullScreenPhoto(photo:    Photo,
dismissAction: @escaping () -> Void) {
        // Present the photo in full-screen
        let           fullScreenVC            =
FullScreenViewController(photo: photo)
        fullScreenVC.dismissAction            =
dismissAction
        present(fullScreenVC,   animated:   true,
completion: nil)
    }
}
```

In this example:

- The `PhotoGalleryViewController` holds a strong reference to `photos`, which are instances of the `Photo` class.
- When displaying a photo in full-screen, we use `[weak self]` in the closure to avoid a retain cycle between the view controller and the closure.

Step 3: Full-Screen View Controller

swift

```
class FullScreenViewController: UIViewController
{
    var photo: Photo
    var dismissAction: (() -> Void)?

    init(photo: Photo) {
        self.photo = photo
        super.init(nibName: nil, bundle: nil)
    }

    required init?(coder: NSCoder) {
        fatalError("init(coder:) has not been
implemented")
    }

    override func viewDidLoad() {
        super.viewDidLoad()

        // Display the photo
```

259

```
        let   imageView   =   UIImageView(image:
photo.image)
        view.addSubview(imageView)

        // Add a dismiss button
        let   dismissButton   =   UIButton(type:
.system)
        dismissButton.setTitle("Dismiss",   for:
.normal)
        dismissButton.addTarget(self,   action:
#selector(dismissTapped), for: .touchUpInside)
        view.addSubview(dismissButton)
    }

    @objc func dismissTapped() {
        dismissAction?()   // Call the dismiss
action
    }
}
```

Summary

In this chapter, we covered:

- **Memory Management in Swift**: Using **Automatic Reference Counting (ARC)** to manage memory automatically in Swift.

- **Strong, Weak, and Unowned References**: Understanding the difference between these references and how they affect memory management.
- **Avoiding Memory Leaks**: How to avoid retain cycles, particularly when using closures and objects with strong references to each other.
- **Example**: We managed memory in a photo gallery app by using weak references in closures to prevent memory leaks.

Proper memory management is essential for building efficient, high-performance apps. In the next chapter, we will explore **handling background tasks** in iOS, such as downloading data or processing tasks in the background.

CHAPTER 24

DEPLOYING YOUR IOS APP

In this chapter, we will guide you through the process of deploying your **iOS app** to the **App Store**. Deployment is the final step of the app development cycle, where your app is made available to users worldwide. You'll learn how to set up your **Apple Developer account**, create **provisioning profiles**, and prepare your app for submission to the **App Store**. We'll also discuss best practices for app deployment and take you through the process of submitting a simple app to the App Store.

Setting Up Your Developer Account and Provisioning Profiles

Before you can deploy an app, you need an **Apple Developer account** and the appropriate **provisioning profiles**. These are required to build and submit apps to the App Store.

1. Apple Developer Account:

To distribute apps on the App Store, you need to sign up for an **Apple Developer account**. The account allows you to access tools, resources, and documentation for iOS development.

- **Cost**: The Apple Developer Program costs $99 per year.

- **Sign-Up**: You can sign up for the Apple Developer Program through the **Apple Developer website** (https://developer.apple.com). You'll need to sign in with your Apple ID and follow the steps to enroll.

Once you've signed up, you can use your developer account to:

- Create and manage certificates for signing apps.
- Configure provisioning profiles.
- Submit your app to the App Store.

2. Provisioning Profiles:

A **provisioning profile** is a collection of settings that allows your app to run on devices and be submitted to the App Store. It includes your app's signing certificate and the devices or app store account it can be installed on.

- **Development Profile**: Allows you to run the app on devices for testing.
- **Distribution Profile**: Used for submitting apps to the App Store.

To create provisioning profiles:

1. Log into the **Apple Developer Portal** (https://developer.apple.com/account).

2. Under **Certificates, Identifiers & Profiles**, select **Provisioning Profiles**.

3. Click the **plus sign** to create a new provisioning profile.

4. Select **App Store** as the distribution method.

5. Choose the app's **App ID** and the correct **distribution certificate**.

The provisioning profile links the app's certificate, app ID, and deployment settings.

Preparing Your App for Submission to the App Store

Before submitting your app, you need to ensure that it meets Apple's guidelines and is prepared correctly for submission.

1. Check App Requirements:

Apple has strict guidelines for apps submitted to the App Store. Make sure your app:

- Complies with **App Store Review Guidelines** (https://developer.apple.com/app-store/review/guidelines/).
- Has a **privacy policy** and does not violate user privacy.
- Uses **appropriate app icons** and **screenshots** for its App Store listing.
- Is **optimized** for various devices and screen sizes.

2. Set Up App Metadata in App Store Connect:

You need to provide various details about your app in **App Store Connect** (https://appstoreconnect.apple.com) for the submission.

Here are the steps:

1. **Sign in** to **App Store Connect** with your Apple Developer credentials.
2. Click on **My Apps** and click the **plus (+) button** to add a new app.
3. Fill in the required metadata:
   o **App Name**: The name of your app.
   o **App Description**: A brief description of your app.
   o **Keywords**: Keywords to improve app discoverability.
   o **App Category**: Choose the appropriate category for your app.
   o **Privacy Policy URL**: If your app collects user data, provide a privacy policy URL.
4. Add **app screenshots** for various device types (iPhone, iPad, etc.). You'll need to provide screenshots that show your app's UI and functionality.

3. Versioning:

Each app you submit to the App Store is assigned a version number. Increment the version number when submitting updates. The version number should follow the format:

- **Major.Minor.Patch** (e.g., 1.0.0 → 1.1.0 for minor updates).

4. Build Settings:

Ensure that your app is using the correct build configuration:

- Set the **Deployment Target** in Xcode to the lowest iOS version your app supports.
- Use **automatic signing** in Xcode, or configure manual signing with the correct provisioning profile and certificate.

Best Practices for App Deployment and Submitting to the App Store

Submitting an app to the App Store requires careful attention to detail. Here are some best practices to follow:

1. Test Your App Thoroughly:

Before submission, make sure your app has been thoroughly tested on different devices and iOS versions. Use **Xcode simulators** to test on various screen sizes and real devices for optimal results.

- **Test on Real Devices**: Make sure your app works well on actual devices.
- **Test Network Conditions**: Check how your app behaves under varying network conditions, such as slow or no internet.

2. Optimize Performance:

Ensure that your app is optimized for performance. This includes:

- Minimizing memory usage.
- Reducing load times.
- Ensuring smooth animations and transitions.

Use **Xcode Instruments** (e.g., **Time Profiler**, **Allocations**, and **Leaks**) to profile your app's performance and detect issues.

3. App Icon and Launch Screen:

- **App Icon**: Ensure that your app icon is clear and well-designed. It must meet the App Store's size requirements (1024x1024).
- **Launch Screen**: Provide a simple and clean launch screen. Avoid excessive text or animations in the launch screen.

4. App Store Guidelines:

Ensure your app adheres to Apple's **App Store Review Guidelines** to avoid rejection during the review process.

Example: Submitting a Simple App to the App Store

Now let's go through the steps of submitting a **simple iOS app** to the App Store.

Step 1: Finalize Your App in Xcode

- Ensure that your app is ready for submission and does not contain any placeholder content.
- Clean up your code and remove any debugging tools or development logs.

Step 2: Archive Your App in Xcode

1. In **Xcode**, select **Product > Archive** to build your app.
2. Once the archive is complete, the **Organizer** window will appear.
3. Click **Distribute App** and select **App Store Connect**.
4. Choose **Upload** to send your app to App Store Connect.

Step 3: Submit via App Store Connect

1. After uploading the app, return to **App Store Connect**.
2. Under **My Apps**, select your app and click **Submit for Review**.
3. Review your app's metadata, screenshots, and version number.
4. Once everything is correct, click **Submit** to send your app for review.

Step 4: Wait for Review

- After submission, your app will be reviewed by Apple's App Review team. This process can take anywhere from a few days to over a week.
- Apple may ask for changes or additional information before approving your app.

Step 5: App Release

- Once approved, you can release your app immediately or schedule a release date.
- Your app will be available for download on the App Store!

Summary

In this chapter, we covered:

- **Setting Up Your Developer Account**: How to sign up for an Apple Developer account and create provisioning profiles for app distribution.
- **Preparing for App Submission**: Ensuring your app meets App Store requirements and setting up metadata in App Store Connect.
- **Best Practices**: Tips for testing, optimizing performance, and adhering to Apple's guidelines for smooth app submission.
- **Submitting to the App Store**: Step-by-step instructions for uploading, submitting, and releasing your app on the App Store.

Successfully deploying your app requires attention to detail, but following the steps outlined in this chapter will ensure that your app is ready for submission and will have the best chance of approval. In the next chapter, we will explore **app updates** and how to manage them once your app is live.